Robert Burns

Selected by
Donald A. Low

PHOENIX

This edition first published in 2010
Phoenix edition first published in 2003

Selection © J. M. Dent 1996
Chronology © J. M. Dent 2003

Typeset by Deltatype Ltd
Birkenhead, Merseyside

Printed in Great Britain by
Clays Ltd, St Ives plc

A CIP catalogue reference for this book
is available from the British Library.

The Orion Publishing Group
Orion House
5 Upper St Martin's Lane
London
WC2H 9EA

Contents

Poems

Robert Burns

The Twa Dogs, A Tale

'Twas in that place o' Scotland's isle,
That bears the name o' auld king COIL,
And aft he's prest, and aft he ca's it guid;
The frugal Wifie, garrulous, will tell,
Upon a bonie day in June,
When wearing thro' the afternoon,
Twa Dogs, that were na thrang at hame,   busy
Forgather'd ance upon a time.

  The first I'll name, they ca'd him *Caesar*,
Was keepet for His Honor's pleasure;
His hair, his size, his mouth, his lugs,   ears
Shew'd he was nane o' Scotland's dogs,
But whalpet some place far abroad,   whelped
Where sailors gang to fish for Cod.

  His locked, letter'd, braw brass-collar
Shew'd him the *gentleman* an' *scholar*;
But tho' he was o' high degree,
The fient a pride na pride had he,   not a bit of
But wad hae spent an hour caressan,
Ev'n wi' a Tinkler-gipsey's *messan*:   mongrel
At Kirk or Market, Mill or Smiddie,   church, smithy
Nae tawted *tyke*, tho' e'er sae duddie,   matted cur, ragged
But he wad stan't, as glad to see him,   stood
An' stroan't on stanes an' hillocks wi' him.   watered, stones

  The tither was a *ploughman's collie*,
A rhyming, ranting, raving billie,   merry, fellow
Wha for his friend an' comrade had him,
And in his freaks had *Luath* ca'd him,   odd notions

3

After some dog in[1] *Highland sang*,
Was made lang syne, lord knows how lang.   long ago
He was a gash an' faithfu' *tyke*,   wise, dog
As ever lap a sheugh or dyke.   leapt, ditch, stone
    wall
His honest, sonsie, baws'nt face   pleasant, white-
    striped
Ay gat him friends in ilka place;
His breast was white, his towzie back,   shaggy
Weel clad wi' coat o' glossy black;
His gawsie tail, wi' upward curl,   cheerful
Hung owre his hurdies wi' a swirl.   buttocks

  Nae doubt but they were fain o' ither,   fond of
An' unco pack an' thick thegither;   very intimate
    together
Wi' social nose whyles snuff'd an' snowket;   sniffed, poked about
Whyles mice and modewurks they howket;   moles, dug
Whyles scour'd awa in lang excursion,   ranged
An' worry'd ither in diversion;
Till tir'd at last wi' mony a farce,
They set them down upon their arse,
An' there began a lang digression
About the *lords o' the creation*.

CAESAR

  I've aften wonder'd, honest *Luath*,
What sort o' life poor dogs like you have;
An' when the *gentry's* life I saw,
What way *poor bodies* liv'd ava.   folk, at all

  Our *Laird* gets in his racked rents,
His coals, his kane, an' a' his stents: payment in kind,
    dues
He rises when he likes himsel;

---

[1] Cuchullin's dog in Ossian's *Fingal*.

4

His flunkies answer at the bell;
He ca's his coach; he ca's his horse;
He draws a bonie, silken purse
As lang's my tail, where thro' the steeks,   steeks — stitches
The yellow letter'd *Geordie* keeks.   guinea, peeps

   Frae morn to een it's nought but toiling,   evening
At baking, roasting, frying, boiling;
An' tho' the gentry first are steghan,   cramming
Yet ev'n the *ha' folk* fill their peghan   servants, stomach
Wi' sauce, ragouts, an' sic like trashtrie,   trash
That's little short o' downright wastrie.   waste/extravagance
Our *Whipper-in*, wee, blastet wonner,   hunt-servant,
Poor worthless elf, it eats a dinner,   wonder
Better than ony *Tenant-man*
His Honor has in a' the lan':
An' what poor *Cot-folk* pit their painch in,   cottagers, put,
I own it's past my comprehension.   paunch

LUATH

   Trowth, Caesar, whyles they're fash't enough;   indeed, troubled
A *Cotter* howkan in a sheugh,
Wi' dirty stanes biggan a dyke.   building
Bairan a quarry, an' sic like,   clearing
Himsel, a wife, he thus sustains
A smytrie o' wee, duddie weans,   swarm, children
An' nought but his han'-daurk, to keep   labour of his hands
Them right an' tight in thack an' raep.   thatch and rope

   An' when they meet wi' sair disasters,   sore
Like loss o' health or want o' masters,
Ye maist wad think, a wee touch langer,
An' they maun starve o' cauld and hunger:

5

But how it comes, I never kent yet,
They're maistly wonderfu' contented;
An' buirdly chiels, and clever hizzies,   *well-built lads,*
Are bred in sic a way as this is.   *wenches*

CAESAR

But then, to see how ye're negleket,
How huff'd, an' cuff'd, an' disrespeket!   *scolded*
L—d man, our gentry care as little
For *delvers*, *ditchers*, an' sic cattle;   *beasts*
They gang as saucy by poor folk,
As I wad by a stinkan brock.   *badger*

I've notic'd, on our Laird's *court-day*,   *rent-day*
An' mony a time my heart's been wae,   *sad*
Poor *tenant bodies*, scant o' cash,
How they maun thole a *factor's* snash;   *endure, insolence*

He'll stamp an' threaten, curse an' swear,
He'll *apprehend* them, *poind* their gear;   *seize, distrain*
While they maun stan', wi' aspect humble,
An' hear it a', an' fear an' tremble!

I see how folk live that hae riches;
But surely poor-folk maun be wretches!

LUATH

They're no sae wretched's ane wad think;   *as one would*
Tho' constantly on poortith's brink,   *poverty*
They're sae accustom'd wi' the sight,
The view o't gies them little fright.

Then chance and fortune are sae guided,
They're ay in less or mair provided;
And tho' fatigu'd wi' close employment,
A blink o' rest's a sweet enjoyment.

The dearest comfort o' their lives,
Their grushie weans an faithfu' wives;   thriving
The *prattling things* are just their pride,
That sweetens a' their fire side.

An' whyles twalpennie-worth o' *nappy* twelvepenny, ale
Can mak the bodies unco happy;   folk
They lay aside their private cares,
To mind the Kirk and State affairs;
They'll talk o' *patronage* an' *priests*,
Wi' kindling fury i' their breasts,
Or tell what new taxation's comin,
An' ferlie at the folk in LON'ON.   marvel

As bleak-fac'd Hallowmass returns,
They get the jovial, rantan *Kirns*,   harvest-homes
When *rural life*, of ev'ry station,
Unite in common recreation;
Love blinks, Wit slaps, an' social Mirth
Forgets there's *care* upo' the earth.

That *merry day* the year begins,
They bar the door on frosty win's;
The nappy reeks wi' mantling ream,   smokes, foam
An' sheds a heart-inspiring steam;
The luntan pipe, an' sneeshin mill,   smoking, snuff-box
Are handed round wi' right guid will; lively, talking
The cantie, auld folks, crackan crouse, cheerfully
The young anes rantan thro' the house – romping

My heart has been sae fain to see them,   *glad*
That I for joy hae barket wi' them.

  Still it's owre true that ye hae said,
Sic game is now owre aften play'd;   *often*
There's monie a creditable *stock*
O' decent, honest, fawsont folk,   *respectable*
Are riven out baith root an' branch,   *torn*
Some rascal's pridefu' greed to quench,
Wha thinks to knit himsel the faster
In favor wi' some *gentle Master*,
Wha aiblins thrang a *parliamentin*,   *perhaps*
For Britain's guid his saul indentin –   *soul, pledging*

CAESAR

  Haith lad ye little ken about it;   'a petty oath' (B)
For Britain's guid! guid faith! I doubt it.
Say rather, gaun as PREMIERS lead him,   *going*
An' saying *aye* or *no's* they bid him:
At Operas an' Plays parading,
Mortgaging, gambling, masquerading:
Or maybe, in a frolic daft,
To HAGUE or CALAIS takes a waft,   *sea-trip*
To make a *tour* an' tak a whirl,   *go on the Grand*
To learn *bon ton* an' see the worl'.   *Tour*

  There, at VIENNA or VERSAILLES,
He rives his father's auld entails;   *splits, estate*
                                                  succession
Or by MADRID he takes the rout,   *road*
To thrum *guittars* an' fecht wi' nowt;   *fight, cattle*
Or down *Italian Vista* startles,
Wh-re-hunting amang groves o' myrtles:
Then bowses drumlie *German-water*,   *boozes, cloudy*

To mak himsel look fair and fatter,
An' purge the bitter ga's an' cankers,   galls
O' curst *Venetian* b-res an' ch-ncres.   cracks, ulcers

For *Britain's guid!* for her destruction!
Wi' dissipation, feud an' faction!

LUATH

Hech man! dear sirs! is that the gate,   way
They waste sae mony a braw estate!
Are we sae foughten and harass'd   worn out
For gear to gang that gate at last!   wealth

O would they stay aback frae courts,
An' please themsels wi' countra sports,
It wad for ev'ry ane be better,
The *Laird*, the *Tenant*, an' the *Cotter*!
For thae frank, rantan, ramblan billies,   these
Fient haet o' them's ill hearted fellows;   not one
Except for breakin o' their timmer,   timber
Or speakin lightly o' their *Limmer*,   mistress
Or shootin of a hare or moorcock,
The ne'er-a-bit they're ill to poor folk.   not in the least

But will ye tell me, master *Caesar*,
Sure *great folk's* life's a life o' pleasure?
Nae cauld nor hunger e'er can steer them,   affect
The vera thought o't need na fear them.   frighten

9

CAESAR

L——d man, were ye but whyles where I am,
The *gentles* ye wad ne'er envy them!   'great folks' (B)

It's true, they need na starve or sweat,
Thro' Winter's cauld, or Summer's heat;
They've nae sair-wark to craze their banes,   hard work,bones
An' fill *auld-age* wi' grips an' granes;   gripes and groans
But *human-bodies* are sic fools,
For a' their colledges an' schools,
That when nae *real* ills perplex them,
They *mak* enow themsels to vex them;   enough
An' ay the less they hae to sturt them,   trouble
In like proportion, less will hurt them.

A country fellow at the pleugh,   plough
His *acre's* till'd, he's right eneugh;
A country girl at her wheel,
Her *dizzen's* done, she's unco weel;   dozen cuts of yarn
But Gentlemen, an' Ladies warst,   worst of all
Wi' ev'n down *want o'wark* are curst.   sheer lack of work
They loiter, lounging, lank an' lazy;
Tho' deil-haet ails them, yet uneasy;   damn-all
Their days, insipid, dull an' tasteless,
Their nights, unquiet, lang an' restless.

An ev'n their sports, their balls an' races,
Their galloping thro' public places,
There's sic parade, sic pomp an' art,
The joy can scarcely reach the heart.

                                                         fall out, card-
                                                         contests
The *Men* cast out in *party-matches*,
Then sowther a' in deep debauches.
Ae night, they're mad wi' drink an' wh-ring,
Niest day their life is past enduring.   next

10

The *Ladies* arm-in-arm in clusters,
As great an' gracious a' as sisters;
But hear their *absent thoughts* o' ither,
They're a' run deils an' jads thegither.   all complete hussies

Whyles, owre the wee bit cup an' platie,
They sip the *scandal-potion* pretty;
Or lee-lang nights, wi' crabbet leuks,   live-long, cross looks

Por owre the devil's *pictur'd beuks*;   playing-cards
Stake on a chance a farmer's stackyard,
An' cheat like ony *unhang'd blackguard*.

  There's some exceptions, man an' woman;
But this is Gentry's life in common.

  By this, the sun was out o' sight,
An' darker gloamin brought the night: twilight
The *bum-clock* humm'd wi' lazy drone,   beetle
The kye stood rowtan i' the loan;   cattle, lowing,
When up they gat an' shook their lugs,   pasture
Rejoic'd they were na *men* but *dogs*;
And each took off his several way,
Resolv'd to meet some ither day.

Scotch Drink

Gie him strong Drink until he wink,
  That's sinking in despair;
An' liquor guid to fire his bluid,
  That's prest wi' grief an' care:
There let him bowse an' deep carouse,
  Wi' bumpers flowing o'er,
Till he forgets his loves or debts
  An' minds his griefs no more.
    Solomon's Proverbs, xxxi. 6, 7

Let other Poets raise a fracas
'Bout vines, an' wines, an' drunken Bacchus,
An' crabbed names an' stories wrack us,   ill-natured
              An' grate our lug,   ear
I sing the juice *Scotch bear* can mak us,   barley
              In glass or jug.

O thou, my MUSE! guid, auld SCOTCH-DRINK!   twisting tubes,
Whether thro' wimplin worms thou jink,   slip fast
Or, richly brown, ream owre the brink,   froth
              In glorious faem,   foam
Inspire me, till I lisp an' wink,
              To sing thy name!

Let husky Wheat the haughs adorn,   level land by a river

And Aits set up their awnie horn,   oats, bearded
An' Pease an' Beans, at een or morn,   evening
              Perfume the plain,
Leeze me on thee John Barleycorn,   you delight me
              Thou king o'grain!

On thee aft Scotland chows her cood,   chews, cud
In souple scones, the wale o' food!   pliable, choice

12

Or tumbling in the boiling flood
  Wi' kail an' beef;   vegetable broth
But when thou pours thy strong *heart's
  blood*,
    There thou shines chief.

Food fills the wame, an' keeps us livin;   stomach
Tho' life's a gift no worth receivin,
When heavy-dragg'd wi' pine an' grievin;
   But oil'd by thee,
The wheels o' life gae down-hill, scrievin,   gliding swiftly
  Wi' rattlin glee.

Thou chears the head o' doited Lear;   stupefied learning
Thou chears the heart o' drooping Care;
Thou strings the nerves o' Labor-sair,   -hard
  At's weary toil;
Thou ev'n brightens dark Despair,
  Wi' gloomy smile.

Aft, clad in massy, siller weed,   silver dress
Wi' Gentles thou erects thy head;   'great folks' (B)
Yet humbly kind, in time o' need,
  The *poor man's* wine;
His wee drap pirratch, or his bread,   drop of, porridge
  Thou kitchens fine.   seasons

Thou art the life o' public haunts;
But thee, what were our fairs and rants?   without, sprees
Ev'n godly meetings o' the saunts,   saints/'the elect'
  By thee inspir'd,
When gaping they besiege the *tents*,   'field pulpit' (B)
  Are doubly fir'd.

That *merry* *night* we get the corn in,
O sweetly, then, thou reams the horn in!   horn vessel
Or reekan on a *New-year-mornin*   smoking
          In cog or bicker,   wooden drinking
                                                      cups
An' just a wee drap *sp'ritual* burn in,   water used in
                                                      brewing
          An gusty sucker!   tasty sugar

When Vulcan gies his bellys breath,
An' Ploughmen gather wi' their graith,   ploughing gear
O rare! to see thee fizz an' freath   froth
          I' the lugget caup!   wood-dish with
                                                      handles
Then *Burnewin* comes on like Death   'burn-wind'/black-
          At ev'ry chap.   smith
                                                    stroke

Nae mercy, then, for airn or steel;   iron
The brawnie, banie, ploughman-chiel   bony, -lad
Brings hard owrehip, wi' sturdy wheel,   over the hip
          The strong forehammer,   sledge-hammer
Till block an' studdie ring an' reel   anvil
          Wi' dinsome clamour.   noisy

When skirlin weanies see the light,   yelling infants
Thou maks the gossips clatter bright,   neighbour-women
                                                    chatter
How fumbling coofs their dearies slight,   clowns
          Wae worth them for't!   cursed be
While healths gae round to him wha, *tight*,   virile
          Gies famous sport.   gives

When neebors anger at a plea,   neighbours
An' just as wud as wud can be,   angry
How easy can the *barley-brie*   whisky
          Cement the quarrel!
It's aye the cheapest Lawyer's fee
          To taste the barrel.

14

Alake! that e'er my *Muse* has reason,
To wyte her countrymen wi' treason!   blame
But monie daily weet their weason   wet, gullet
            Wi' liquors nice,
An' hardly, in a winter season,
            E'er spier her price.   ask

Wae worth that *Brandy*, burnan trash!
Fell source o' monie a pain an' brash!   severe, illness
Twins monie a poor, doylt, druken hash   deprives, muddled,
            O' half his days;   drunken waster
An' sends, beside, auld *Scotland's* cash
            To her warst faes.   worst foes

Ye Scots wha wish auld Scotland well,
Ye chief, to you my tale I tell,
Poor, plackless devils like *mysel*,   penniless
            It sets you ill,
Wi' bitter, dearthfu' *wines* to mell,   meddle
            Or foreign gill.   measure

May *Gravels* round his blather wrench,   urinary pains,
An' *Gouts* torment him, inch by inch,   bladder
Wha twists his gruntle wi' a glunch   snout, frown
            O' sour disdain,
Out owre a glass o' *Whisky-punch*
            Wi' honest men!

O *Whisky!* soul o' plays an' pranks!
Accept a *Bardie's* gratefu' thanks!   poet's
When wanting thee, what tuneless cranks   noises
            Are my poor Verses!
Thou comes – they rattle i' their ranks
            At ither's arses!

15

Thee Ferintosh! O sadly lost!   a whisky
Scotland lament frae coast to coast!
Now colic-grips, an' barkin hoast,   cough
          May kill us a';
Fo loyal Forbes' *Charter'd boast*
          Is ta'en awa!

Thae curst horse-leeches o' th'Excise,   those
Wha mak the *Whisky stells* their prize!   stills
Haud up thy han' *Diel!* ance, twice, *thrice!* hold, Devil
          There, seize the blinkers!   spies/cheats
An' bake them up in brunstane pies   brimstone
          For poor d—n'd *Drinkers*.

Fortune, if thou'll but gie me still   give
Hale breeks, a scone, an' *whisky gill*,   intact breeches
An' rowth o' rhyme to rave at will,   abundance
          Tak a' the rest,
An' deal't about as thy blind skill
          Directs thee best.

The Holy Fair

A robe of seeming truth and trust
  Hid crafty observation;
And secret hung, with poison'd crust,
  The dirk of Defamation:
A mask that like the gorget show'd,
  Dye-varying, on the pigeon;
And for a mantle large and broad,
  He wrapt him in Religion.

          Hypocrisy A-La-Mode

I

Upon a simmer Sunday morn,   summer
  When Nature's face is fair,
I walked forth to view the corn,
  An' snuff the callor air.   sniff, fresh
The rising sun, owre GALSTON Muirs,   over
  Wi' glorious light was glintan;
The hares were hirplan down the furrs,   moving unevenly
                                                   forward, furrows
  The lav'rocks they were chantan   larks
          Fu' sweet that day.   very

II

As lightsomely I glowr'd abroad   gazed intently
  To see a scene sae gay,
Three *hizzies*, early at the road,   wenches
  Cam skelpan up the way.   hurrying
Twa had manteeles o' dolefu' black,   capes
  But ane wi' lyart lining;   grey
The third, that gaed a wee a-back,   a little in the rear
  Was in the fashion shining
          Fu' gay that day.

17

III

The twa appear'd like sisters twin,
  In feature, form an' claes;   *clothes*
Their visage wither'd, lang an' thin,
  An' sour as ony slaes: *sloes*
The third cam up, hap-step-an'-loup,   *hop-step-and-jump*
  As light as ony lambie,   *little lamb*
An' wi' a curchie low did stoop,   *curtsy*
  As soon as e'er she saw me,
        Fu' kind that day.

IV

Wi' bonnet aff, quoth I, 'Sweet lass,
  I think ye seem to ken me;
I'm sure I've seen that bonie face,
  But yet I canna name ye.'
Quo' she, an' laughan as she spak,   *said, spoke*
  An' taks me by the han's,   *hands*
'Ye, for my sake, hae gien the feck   *have given most*
  Of a' the ten comman's   *commandments*
        A screed some day.'   *tear/rent*

V

'My name is FUN – your cronie dear,
  The nearest friend ye hae;
An' this is SUPERSTITION here,
  An' that's HYPOCRISY.
I'm gaun to ********* holy fair,   *[Mauchline]*
  To spend an hour in daffin: *frolic*
Gin ye'll go there, yon runkl'd pair,   *if, that wrinkled*
  We will get famous laughin
        At them this day.'

VI

Quoth I, 'With a' my heart, I'll do't;
  I'll get my Sunday's sark on,   shirt
An' meet you on the holy spot;
  Faith, we'se hae fine remarkin!'   we'll, entertainment

Then I gaed hame at crowdie-time,   breakfast-time
  An' soon I made me ready;
For roads were clad, frae side to side,
  Wi' monie a wearie body,   person
        In droves that day.

VII

Here, farmers gash, in ridin graith,   smart, habit
  Gaed hoddan by their cotters;   jogging, cottagers
There, swankies young, in braw braid-claith,   strapping lads,
  Are springan owre the gutters.   broad-cloth
The lasses, skelpan barefit, thrang,   hurrying, barefoot in
  In silks an' scarlets glitter;   a crowd
Wi' *sweet-milk cheese*, in monie a whang,   thick slice
  An' *farls*, bak'd wi' butter,   bits of oaten
        Fu' crump that day.   bannock
                              'hard and brittle' (B)

VIII

When by the *plate* we set our nose,
  Weel heaped up wi' ha'pence,
A greedy glowr *Black-bonnet* throws,
  An' we maun draw our tippence.   twopence
Then in we go to see the show,
  On ev'ry side they're gath'ran;
Some carryan dails, some chairs an' stools,   deal planks
  An' some are busy bleth'ran   chatting hard
        Right loud that day.

IX

Here stands a shed to fend the show'rs,
    An' screen our countra Gentry;
There, *Racer Jess*, an' twathree wh-res,   two or three
    Are blinkan at the entry.
Here sits a raw o' tittlan jads,   row, gossiping
    Wi' heaving breasts an' bare neck;   hussies
An' there, a batch o' *Wabster lads*,   weaver
    Blackguarding frae K*******ck   roistering,
          For fun this day.   [Kilmarnock]

X

Here, some are thinkan on their sins,
    An' some upo' their claes;
Ane curses feet that fyl'd his shins,   fouled
    Anither sighs an' prays:
On this hand sits an *Elect* swatch,   sample
    Wi' screw'd-up, grace-proud faces;   sanctimonious
On that, a set o' chaps, at watch,
    Thrang winkan on the lasses   throng
          To *chairs* that day.

XI

O happy is that man, an' blest!
    Nae wonder that it pride him!
Whase ain dear lass, that he likes best,   own
    Comes clinkan down beside him!   sitting smartly
Wi' arm repos'd on the *chair-back*,
    He sweetly does compose him;
Which, by degrees, slips round her *neck*
    An's loof upon her *bosom*   palm
          Unkend that day.

XII

Now a' the congregation o'er
  Is silent expectation;
For ****** speels the holy door,   [Moodie] climbs
  Wi' tidings o' s-lv-t—n.
Should *Hornie*, as in ancient days,   Satan
  'Mang sons o' G— present him,
The vera sight o' ******'s face,
  To's ain *het hame* had sent him   hot home (Hell)
        Wi' fright that day.

XIII

Hear how he clears the points o' Faith
  Wi' rattlin an' thumpin!
Now meekly calm, now wild in wrath,
  He's stampan, an' he's jumpan!
His lengthen'd chin, his turn'd up snout,
  His eldritch squeel an' gestures,   hideous
O how they fire the heart devout,
  Like *cantharidian* plaisters
        On sic a day!

XIV

But hark! the *tent* has chang'd its voice;   'field pulpit' (B)
  There's peace an' rest nae langer;
For a' the *real judges* rise,
  They canna sit for anger.
***** opens out his cauld harangues,   [Smith]
  On *practice* and on *morals*,
An' aff the *godly* pour in thrangs,
  To gie the jars an' barrels
        A lift that day.

21

XV

What signifies his barren shine,
    Of moral pow'rs an' reason?
His English style, an' gesture fine,
    Are a' clean out o' season.
Like SOCRATES or ANTONINE,
    Or some auld pagan heathen,
The moral man he does define,
    But ne'er a word o' faith in
            That's right that day.

XVI

In guid time comes an antidote
    Against sic poosion'd nostrum;   poisoned remedy
For *******, frae the water-fit,   [Peebles], river-
    Ascends the holy rostrum: mouth
See, up he's got the word o' G—,
    An' meek an' mim has view'd it,   demure
While COMMON-SENSE has taen the road,
    An' aff, an' up the Cowgate
            Fast, fast that day.

XVII

Wee ****** niest the Guard relieves,   [Miller], next
    An' Orthodoxy raibles,   gabbles
Tho' in his heart he weel believes,
    An' thinks it auld wives' fables:
But faith! the birkie wants a Manse,   fellow
    So, cannilie he hums them;   dextrously, takes
Altho' his carnal Wit an' Sense   them in
    Like hafflins-wise o'ercomes him   in half measure/partly
            At times that day.

XVIII

Now, butt an' ben, the Change-house fills,   *in outer and inner room, tavern*
    Wi' *yill-caup* Commentators: *ale-cup*
Here's crying out for bakes an' gills,   *biscuits, drams*
    An' there the pint-stowp clatters;   *-measure*
While thick an' thrang, an' loud an' lang,   *closely engaged*
    Wi' *Logic*, an' wi' *Scripture*,   *together*
They raise a din, that, in the end,
    Is like to breed a rupture
          O' wrath that day.

XIX

Leeze me on Drink! it gies us mair   *I'm all for*
    Than either School or Colledge:
It kindles Wit, it waukens Lear,   *wakens Learning*
    It pangs us fou o' Knowledge.   *stuffs, full*
Be't *whisky-gill* or *penny-wheep*,   *small beer*
    Or ony stronger potion,
It never fails, on drinkin deep,
    To kittle up our *notion*,   *rouse, fancy*
          By night or day.

XX

The lads an' lasses, blythely bent
    To mind baith *saul* an' *body*,   *soul*
Sit round the table, weel content,   *whisky, hot*
    An' steer about the *toddy*.   *water and sugar*
On this ane's dress, an' that ane's leuk,   *expression*
    They're makin observations;
While some are cozie i' the neuk,   *corner*
    An' forming *assignations*
          To meet some day.

XXI

But now the L—'s ain trumpet touts,   blasts
  Till a' the hills are rairan,   roaring
An' echoes back return the shouts;
  Black ****** is na spairan: [Russel], sparing
His piercin words, like Highlan swords,
  Divide the joints an' marrow;
His talk o' H-ll, where devils dwell,
  Our vera[1] 'Sauls does harrow'
        Wi' fright that day!

XXII

A vast, unbottom'd, boundless Pit,
  Fill'd fou o' *lowan brunstane*,   blazing
                             brimstone
Whase raging flame, an' scorching heat,
  Wad melt the hardest whun-stane!   whinstone
The *half asleep* start up wi' fear,
  An' think they hear it roaran,
When presently it does appear,
  'Twas but some neebor *snoran*   neighbour snoring
        Asleep that day.

XXIII

'Twad be owre lang a tale to tell,
  How monie stories past,
An' how they crouded to the yill,   crowded, ale
  When they were a' dismist:
How drink gaed round, in cogs an' caups,   dishes, bowls
  Amang the furms an' benches;   forms
An' *cheese* an' *bread*, frae women's laps,
  Was dealt about in lunches,
        An' dawds that day.   hunks

[1] Shakespeare's *Hamlet*.

24

XXIV

In comes a gawsie, gash *Guidwife*,   jovial, neat matron
  An' sits down by the fire,
Syne draws her *kebbuck* an' her knife;   then, cheese
  The lasses they are shyer.
The auld *Guidmen*, about the *grace*,   husbands
  Frae side to side they bother,
Till some ane by his bonnet lays,
  An' gies them't, like a *tether*,   rope
        Fu' lang that day.   very

XXV

Waesucks! for him that gets nae lass,   alas
  Or lasses that hae naething!
Sma' need has he to say a grace,   'soil with meal' (B)
  Or melvie his braw claithing!   clothing
O *Wives* be mindfu', ance yoursel,
  How bonie lads ye wanted,
An' dinna, for a *kebbuck-heel*,   do not, heel of
  Let lasses be affronted   cheese
        On sic a day!

XXVI

Now *Clinkumbell*, wi' rattlan tow,   bellringer, rope
  Begins to jow an' croon;   toll and sound
Some swagger hame, the best they dow,   are able
  Some wait the afternoon.
At slaps the billies halt a blink,   gaps in dyke, fellows
  Till lasses strip their shoon: shoes
Wi' *faith* an' *hope*, an' *love* an' *drink*,
  They're a' in famous tune
        For crack that day.   chat

25

XXVII

How monie hearts this day converts,
  O' sinners and o' Lasses!
Their hearts o' stane, gin night are gane,   *stone, by nightfall gone*
  As saft as ony flesh is.   *soft*
There's some are fou o' *love divine*;
  There's some are fou o' *brandy*;
An' monie jobs that day begin,   *intrigues*
  May end in *Houghmagandie*   *fornication*
      Some ither day.

Address to the Deil

O Prince, O chief of many throned pow'rs,
That led th'embattl'd Seraphim to war —

Milton

O Thou, whatever title suit thee!
Auld Hornie, Satan, Nick, or Clootie,   Cloven-hoof
Wha in yon cavern grim an' sootie,
      Clos'd under hatches,
Spairges about the brunstane cootie,   bespatters,
                      brimstone tub
      To scaud poor wretches!   scald

Hear me, *auld Hangie*, for a wee,   Hangman
An' let poor, *damned bodies* bee;
I'm sure sma' pleasure it can gie,
      Ev'n to a *deil*,   devil
To skelp an' scaud poor dogs like me,   smack
      An' hear us squeel!

Great is thy pow'r, an' great thy fame;
Far kend an' noted is thy name;
An' tho' yon *lowan heugh's* thy hame,   blazing pit
      Thou travels far;
An' faith! thou's neither lag nor lame,   backward
      Nor blate nor scaur.   bashful, afraid

Whyles, ranging like a roaran lion,
For prey, a' holes an' corners tryin;
Whyles, on the strong-wing'd Tempest flyin,
      Tirlan the *kirks*;   uncovering, churches
Whyles, in the human bosom pryin,
      Unseen thou lurks.

I've heard my rev'rend *Graunie* say,   grandmother
In lanely glens ye like to stray;   lonely
Or where auld, ruin'd castles, gray,
       Nod to the moon,
Ye fright the nightly wand'rer's way,
       Wi' eldritch croon.   unearthly moan

When twilight did my *Graunie* summon,
To say her pray'rs, douse, honest woman!   sober
Aft 'yont the dyke she's heard you bumman,   behind, wall,
       Wi' eerie drone;   humming
Or, rustling, thro' the boortries coman,   elder trees
       Wi' heavy groan.

Ae dreary, windy, winter night,
The stars shot down wi' sklentan light,   slanting
Wi' you, *mysel*, I gat a fright,
       Ayont the lough;   beyond, loch
Ye, like a *rash-buss*, stood in sight,   clump of rushes
       Wi' waving sugh.   sound of wind

The cudgel in my neive did shake,   fist
Each bristl'd hair stood like a stake,
When wi' an eldritch, stoor *quaick, quaick*,   harsh
       Amang the springs,
Awa ye squatter'd like a *drake*,   'flutter in water' (B)
       On whistling wings.

Let *Warlocks* grim, an' wither'd *Hags*,
Tell how wi' you on ragweed nags,   ragwort
They skim the muirs an' dizzy crags,   moors
       Wi' wicked speed;
And in kirk-yards renew their leagues,
       Owre howcket dead.   exhumed

Thence, countra wives, wi' toil an' pain,
May plunge an' plunge the kirn in vain;   churn
For Oh! the yellow treasure's taen
        By witching skill;
An' dawtet, twal-pint *Hawkie's* gane   spoiled, twelve-cow
        As yell's the Bill.   milkless as, bull

Thence, mystic knots mak great abuse,
On *Young-Guidmen,* fond, keen an' croose;   -husbands, confident
When the best *wark-lume* i' the house,   work-loom
        By cantraip wit,   magic
Is instant made no worth a louse,
        Just at the bit.   critical moment

When thowes dissolve the snawy hoord,   thaws, snowy drift
An' float the jinglan icy boord,   (on), cracking,
                 surface
Then, *Water-kelpies* haunt the foord,   waterhorse
        By your direction,   demons, ford
An' nighted Trav'llers are allur'd
        To their destruction.

An' aft your moss-traversing *Spunkies*   wills o' the wisp
Decoy the wight that late an' drunk is:
The bleezan, curst, mischievous monkies   blazing
        Delude his eyes,
Till in some miry slough he sunk is,
        Ne'er mair to rise.

When MASONS' mystic *word* an' *grip,*
In storms an' tempests raise you up,
Some cock or cat, your rage maun stop,
        Or, strange to tell!
The *youngest Brother* ye wad whip
        Aff straught to H-ll.   straight

Lang syne in EDEN's bonie yard,   long ago, garden
When youthfu' lovers first were pair'd,
An' all the Soul of Love they shar'd,
        The raptur'd hour,
Sweet on the fragrant, flow'ry swaird,   sward
        In shady bow'r.

Then you, ye auld, snick-drawing dog!   latch-
Ye cam to Paradise incog,   unknown
An' play'd on man a cursed brogue,   trick
        (Black be your fa'!)
An' gied the infant warld a shog,   world, shock
        'Maist ruin'd a'.

D'ye mind that day, when in a bizz,   remember, stir
Wi' reeket duds, an' reestet gizz,   smoky clothes,
Ye did present your smoutie phiz,   'cured' wig
        'Mang better folk,   ugly face
An' sklented on the man of Uzz,   directed aslant
        Your spitefu' joke?

An how ye gat him i' your thrall,
An' brak him out o' house an' hal',
While scabs an' botches did him gall,   'angry tumours' (B)
        Wi' bitter claw,   scratching
An' lows'd his ill-tongu'd, wicked Scawl   loosed, abusive
                                                    woman
        Was warst ava?   worst of all

But a' your doings to rehearse,
Your wily snares an' fechtin fierce,   fighting
Sin' that day[1] MICHAEL did you pierce,
        Down to this time,

---

[1] *Vide* Milton, Book 6th.

Wad ding a' *Lallan* tongue, or *Erse*,   weary, Lowland, Gaelic
    In Prose or Rhyme.

An' now, auld *Cloots*, I ken ye're thinkan,
A certain *Bardie's* rantin, drinkin,   poet
Some luckless hour will send him linkan,   going briskly
    To your black pit;
But faith! he'll turn a corner jinkan,   side-stepping
    An' cheat you yet.

But fare-you-weel, auld *Nickie-ben*!
O wad ye tak a thought an' men'!   and mend
Ye aiblins might – I dinna ken –   perhaps
    Still hae a *stake* –   chance
I'm wae to think upo' yon den,   unhappy
    Ev'n for your sake!

The Death and Dying Words of Poor Mailie,

The Author's Only Pet Yowe, An Unco Mournfu' Tale

As MAILIE, an' her lambs thegither,
Was ae day nibbling on the tether,
Upon her cloot she coost a hitch,   hoof, cast
An' owre she warsl'd in the ditch: struggled
There, groaning, dying, she did ly,
When[1] Hughoc he cam doytan by.   blundering

  Wi' glowrin een, an' lifted han's,   eyes, hands
Poor Hughoc like a statue stan's;
He saw her days were near hand ended,   almost
But, waes my heart! he could na mend it!   woe is
He gaped wide, but naething spak,   spoke
At length poor Mailie silence brak.   broke

  'O thou, whase lamentable face
Appears to mourn my woefu' case!
My dying words attentive hear,
An' bear them to my Master dear.

  'Tell him, if e'er again he keep
As muckle gear as buy a sheep,   money
O, bid him never tye them mair,
Wi' wicked strings o' hemp or hair!
But ca' them out to park or hill,
An' let them wander at their will:
So, may his flock increase an' grow
To scores o' lambs, an' packs of woo'!   wool

[1] A neebor herd-callan.

32

'Tell him, he was a Master kin',   kindly
An' ay was guid to me an' mine;
An' now my *dying* charge I gie him,
My helpless *lambs*, I trust them wi' him.

'O, bid him save their harmless lives,
Frae dogs an' tods, an' butchers' knives!   foxes
But gie them guid *cow-milk* their fill,
Till they be fit to fend themsel;
An' tent them duely, e'en an' morn,   tend
Wi' taets o' *hay* an' ripps o' *corn*.   tufts, handfuls

'An' may they never learn the gaets,   ways
Of ither vile, wanrestfu' *Pets*!   restless
To slink thro' slaps, an' reave an' steal,   gaps, plunder
At stacks o' pease, or stocks o' kail.   green kale
So may they, like their great *forbears*,
For monie a year come thro' the sheers:
So *wives* will gie them bits o' bread,
An' *bairns* greet for them when they're dead.   weep

'My poor *toop-lamb*, my son an' heir,   ram-
O, bid him breed him up wi' care!
An' if he live to be a beast,
To pit some havins in his breast!   put, sense
An' warn him ay at riding time,
To stay content wi' *yowes* at hame;
An' no to rin an' wear his cloots,   run, hooves
Like ither menseless, graceless brutes.   ill-bred, senseless

'An' niest my *yowie*, silly thing,   next, young ewe
Gude keep thee frae a *tether string*!
O, may thou ne'er forgather up,
Wi' onie blastet, moorlan *toop*;   accursed, ram

33

But ay keep mind to moop an' mell,   nibble, mix
Wi' sheep o' credit like thysel!

   'And now, my *bairns*, wi' my last breath,
I lea'e my blessin wi' you baith:
An' when ye think upo' your Mither,   mother
Mind to be kind to ane anither.   remember

   'Now, honest Hughoc, dinna fail,   don't
To tell my Master a' my tale;
An' bid him burn this cursed *tether*,
An' for thy pains thou'se get my blather.'   you will, bladder

   This said, poor *Mailie* turn'd her head,
An' clos'd her een amang the dead!

34

Poor Mailie's Elegy

Lament in rhyme, lament in prose,
Wi' saut tears trickling down your nose;   saut   salt
Our Bardie's fate is at a close,   Bardie's   poet's
   Past a' remead!   remead   cure
The last, sad cape-stane of his woes;   cape-stane   coping-stone
  Poor Mailie's dead!

It's no the loss o' warl's gear,   warl's gear   worldly property
That could sae bitter draw the tear,
Or make our Bardie, dowie, wear   dowie   sad
   The mourning weed:
He's lost a friend and neebor dear,   neebor   neighbour
  In Mailie dead.

Thro' a' the town she trotted by him;   town   village/farm
A lang half-mile she could descry him;
Wi' kindly bleat, when she did spy him,
   She ran wi' speed:
A friend mair faithfu' ne'er came nigh him,
  Than Mailie dead.

I wat she was a sheep o' sense,   wat   know
An' could behave hersel wi' mense: mense   discretion
I'll say't, she never brak a fence,   brak   broke
   Thro' thievish greed.
Our Bardie, lanely, keeps the spence,   lanely, spence lonely, inner room
  Sin' Mailie's dead.

Or, if he wanders up the howe,   howe   valley
Her living image in her yowe,   yowe   ewe
Comes bleating till him, owre the knowe,   till   to
   For bits o' bread;

35

An' down the briny pearls rowe   roll
        For *Mailie* dead.

She was nae get o' moorlan tips,   offspring, tups
Wi' tauted ket, an' hairy hips;   matted fleece
For her forbears were brought in ships,
        Frae 'yont the TWEED: beyond
A bonier *fleesh* ne'er cross'd the clips   fleece, shears
        Than *Mailie's* dead.

Wae worth that man wha first did shape,   woe to
That vile, wanchancie thing – *a raep*!   unlucky, rope
It makes guid fellows girn an' gape,   'twist the features
        Wi' chokin dread;   in rage' (B)
An' *Robin's* bonnet wave wi' crape
        For *Mailie* dead.

O, a' ye *Bards* on bonie DOON!
An' wha on AIRE your chanters tune!
Come, join the melancholious croon   moan
        O' *Robin's* reed!
His heart will never get aboon!   above
        His *Mailie's* dead!

36

To J. S****

Friendship, mysterious cement of the soul!
Sweet'ner of Life, and solder of Society!
I owe thee much —

                    Blair

Dear S****, the sleest, pawkie thief,   cleverest, humorous
That e'er attempted stealth or rief,   plunder
Ye surely hae some warlock-breef   charm/wizard-spell
      Owre human hearts;
For ne'er a bosom yet was prief   proof
      Against your arts.

For me, I swear by sun an' moon,
And ev'ry star that blinks aboon,   above
Ye've cost me twenty pair o' shoon   shoes
      Just gaun to see you;
And ev'ry ither pair that's done,
      Mair taen I'm wi' you.

That auld, capricious carlin, *Nature*,   old woman
To mak amends for scrimpet stature,   stunted
She's turn'd you off, a human-creature
      On her first plan,
And in her freaks, on ev'ry feature,
      She's wrote, *the Man*.

Just now I've taen the fit o' rhyme,
My barmie noddle's working prime,   yeasty brain
My fancy yerket up sublime   stirred
      Wi' hasty summon:
Hae ye a leisure-moment's time
      To hear what's coming?

Some rhyme a neebor's name to lash;   neighbour
Some rhyme, (vain thought!) for needfu'
        cash;
Some rhyme to court the countra clash,   invite, talk
            An' raise a din;
For me, an *aim* I never fash;   bother about
            I rhyme for fun.

The star that rules my luckless lot,
Has fated me the russet coat,   poor man's
                                                        rural wear
An' damn'd my fortune to the groat;   small coin
            But, in requit,   by way of
                                                        compensation
Has blest me with a *random-shot*
        O' countra wit.

This while my notion's taen a sklent,   slant/turn
To try my fate in guid, black *prent*;   print
But still the mair I'm that way bent,   'take leisure,
            Something cries, 'hoolie!   stop!' (B)
I red you, honest man, tak tent!   advise, take care
            Ye'll shaw your folly.   show

'There's ither Poets, much your betters,
Far seen in *Greek*, deep men o' *letters*,   well-versed
Hae thought they had ensur'd their debtors,   insured as
            A' future ages;
Now moths deform in shapeless tatters,
        Their unknown pages.'

Then farewell hopes of Laurel-boughs,
To garland my poetic brows!
Henceforth, I'll rove where busy ploughs
            Are whistling thrang,   busily
An' teach the lanely heights an' howes   lonely, hollows
        My rustic sang.

I'll wander on with tentless heed,   careless
How never-halting moments speed,
Till fate shall snap the brittle thread;
          Then, all unknown,
I'll lay me with th'*inglorious dead*,
          Forgot and gone!

But why, o' Death, begin a tale?
Just now we're living sound an' hale;
Then top and maintop croud the sail,   crowd
          Heave *Care* o'er-side!
And large, before Enjoyment's gale,
          Let's tak the tide.

This life, sae far's I understand,   so far as
Is a' enchanted fairy-land,
Where Pleasure is the Magic-wand
          That, wielded right,
Maks Hours like Minutes, hand in hand,
          Dance by fu' light.   full

The *magic-wand* then let us wield;
For, ance that five an' forty's speel'd,   climbed
See, crazy, weary, joyless Eild,   Old Age
          Wi' wrinkl'd face,
Comes hostan, hirplan owre the field,   coughing, limping
          Wi' creeping pace.

When ance life's *day* draws near the gloamin,   twilight
Then fareweel vacant, careless roamin;
An' fareweel chearfu' tankards foamin,
          An' social noise;
An' fareweel dear, deluding woman,
          The joy of joys!

39

O Life! how pleasant in thy morning,
Young Fancy's rays the hills adorning!
Cold-pausing Caution's lessons scorning,
      We frisk away,
Like school-boys, at th' expected warning,
      To joy and play.

We wander there, we wander here,
We eye the *rose* upon the brier,
Unmindful that the *thorn* is near,
      Among the leaves;
And tho' the puny wound appear,
      Short while it grieves.

Some, lucky, find a flow'ry spot,
For which they never toil'd nor swat;   sweated
They drink the *sweet* and eat the *fat*,
      But care or pain;   without
And haply, eye the barren hut,
      With high disdain.

With steady aim, Some Fortune chase;
Keen hope does ev'ry sinew brace;
Thro' fair, thro' foul, they urge the race,
      And seize the prey:
Then canie, in some cozie place,   cautious,
      They close the *day*.   comfortable

And others, like your humble servan',
Poor wights! nae rules nor roads observin;   fellows
To right or left, eternal swervin,
      They zig-zag on;

40

Till curst with Age, obscure an' starvin,
        They aften groan.

Alas! what bitter toil an' straining –
But truce with peevish, poor complaining!
Is Fortune's fickle *Luna* waning?   Moon
        E'en let her gang!
Beneath what light she has remaining,
        Let's sing our Sang.

My pen I here fling to the door,
And kneel, 'Ye *Pow'rs*', and warm implore,
'Tho' I should wander *Terra* o'er,   Earth
        In all her climes,
Grant me but this, I ask no more,
        Ay rowth o' rhymes.   plenty

'Gie dreeping roasts to *countra Lairds*,   dripping
Till icicles hing frae their beards;   hang
Gie fine braw claes to fine *Life-guards*,   clothes
        And *Maids of Honor*;
And yill an' whisky gie to *Cairds*,   ale, tinkers
        Until they sconner.   feel disgust

'A *Title*, DEMPSTER merits it;
A *Garter* gie to WILLIE PIT;
Gie Wealth to some be-ledger'd Cit,   townsman
        In cent per cent;
But give me real, sterling Wit,
        And I'm content.

'While ye are pleas'd to keep me hale,   healthy
I'll sit down o'er my scanty meal,
Be't *water-brose*, or *muslin-kail*,   -porridge,
                                                       meatless broth

41

        Wi' chearfu' face,
As lang's the Muses dinna fail
        To say the grace.'

An anxious e'e I never throws   eye
Behint my lug, or by my nose;   ear
I jouk beneath Misfortune's blows   dodge
        As weel's I may,
Sworn foe to *sorrow*, *care*, and *prose*,
        I rhyme away.

O ye, douse folk, that live by rule,   sedate
Grave, tideless-blooded, calm and cool,
Compar'd wi' you – O fool! fool! fool!
        How much unlike!
Your hearts are just a standing pool,
        Your lives, a dyke!   stone wall

Nae hare-brain'd, sentimental traces,
In your unletter'd, nameless faces!
In *arioso* trills and graces
        Ye never stray,
But *gravissimo*, solemn basses
        Ye hum away.

Ye are sae *grave*, nae doubt ye're *wise*;
Nae ferly tho' ye do despise   wonder
The hairum-scairum, ram-stam boys,   wild, reckless
        The rambling squad:
I see ye upward cast your eyes –
        – Ye ken the road –

42

Whilst I – but I shall haud me there –   hold
Wi' you I'll scarce gang *only where* –
Then *Jamie*, I shall say nae mair,
      But quat my sang,   end
Content *with* YOU to mak a *pair*,
      Whare'er I gang.

The Auld Farmer's New-Year-Morning Salutation to his Auld Mare, Maggie

On Giving Her the Accustomed Ripp of Corn to Hansel
in the New-Year

A Guid New-Year I wish you Maggie!
Hae, there's a ripp to thy auld baggie: *fist of unthreshed*
                                        corn, belly
Tho' thou's howe-backet, now, an' knaggie,   *'sunk in the back'*
          I've seen the day,   *(B), bony*
Thou could hae gaen like ony staggie   *colt*
              Out owre the lay.   *outfield*

Tho' now thou's dowie, stiff an' crazy,   *sickly, infirm*
An' thy auld hide as white's a daisy,
I've seen thee dappl't, sleek an' glazie,   *glittering smooth*
          A bonie gray: *like glass*
He should been tight that daur't to raize thee,   *capable, dared*
                                          provoke
          Ance in a day.

Thou ance was i' the foremost rank,
A filly buirdly, steeve an' swank,   *stately, strong, agile*
An' set weel down a shapely shank,
          As e'er tread yird;   *earth*
An' could hae flown out owre a stank,   *pool of standing*
          Like onie bird.   *water*

It's now some nine-an'-twenty year,
Sin' thou was my Guidfather's Meere;   *father-in-law's mare*
He gied me thee, o' tocher clear,   *dowry*
          An' fifty mark;
Tho' it was sma', 'twas weel-won gear,   *property*
          An' thou was stark.   *strong*

When first I gaed to woo my *Jenny*,
Ye then was trottan wi' your Minnie;   mother
Tho' ye was trickie, slee an' funnie,   clever
        Ye ne'er was donsie;   ill-tempered
But hamely, tawie, quiet an' cannie,   'that handles
                                                          quietly' (B)
        An' unco sonsie.   tractable

That *day*, ye pranc'd wi' muckle pride,
When ye bure hame my bonie *Bride*:   bore
An' sweet an' gracefu' she did ride
        Wi' maiden air!
KYLE-STEWART I could bragged wide,   have challenged
        For sic a *pair*.

Tho' now ye dow but hoyte and hoble,   can only move
                                                          clumsily
An' wintle like a saumont-coble,   roll, salmon-boat
That day, ye was a jinker noble,   high-spirited beast
        For heels an' win'!   wind
An' ran them till they a' did wauble   wobble
        Far, far behin'!

When thou an' I were young an' skiegh,   mettlesome
An' *Stable-meals* at Fairs were driegh,   dreary
How thou wad prance, an' snore, an' scriegh,   snort, neigh
        An' tak the road!
Towns-bodies ran, an' stood abiegh,   town folk, at a
                                                          shy distance
        An' ca't thee mad.

When thou was corn't, an' I was mellow,   fed with corn
We took the road ay like a Swallow:
At *Brooses* thou had ne'er a fellow,   wedding-races
        For pith an' speed;   energy
But ev'ry tail thou pay't them hollow,   beat
        Whare'er thou gaed.

The sma', droot-rumpl't, hunter cattle,
Might aiblins waur't thee for a brattle;
But *sax Scotch* mile, thou try't their mettle,
          An' gart them whaizle:
Nae whip nor spur, but just a wattle
          O' saugh or hazle.

Thou was a noble *Fittie-lan'*,
As e'er in tug or tow was drawn!
Aft thee an' I, in aught hours gaun,
          On guid March-weather,
Hae turn'd *sax rood* beside our han',
          For days thegither.

Thou never braing't, an' fetch't, an' flisket,
But thy *auld tail* thou wad hae whisket,
An' spread abreed thy weel-fill'd *brisket*,
          Wi' pith an pow'r,
Till sprittie knowes wad rair't an' risket
          An' slypet owre.

When frosts lay lang, an' snaws were deep,
An' threaten'd *labor* back to keep,
I gied thy *cog* a wee-bit heap
          Aboon the timmer;
I ken'd my *Maggie* wad na sleep
          For that, or Simmer.

In *cart* or *car* thou never reestet;
The steyest brae thou wad hae fac't it;
Thou never lap, an' sten't, an' breastet,
          Then stood to blaw;

Glosses (right margin):

with drooping haunches, beasts
perhaps, beat, short race
six

made, wheeze

stick

willow

rear left plough horse

leather or rope

eight

by ourselves

drew unsteadily, gasped, fretted

abroad, breast

rushy hillocks, roared, torn underfoot
fallen

snows

dish

above, wooden edge
without, before
summer

stood restive
stiffest hill
leapt, reared, pulled forward
blow

46

But just thy step a wee thing hastet,
       Thou snoov't awa.   *went steadily on*

My Pleugh is now thy *bairn-time* a';   *plough-team, brood*
Four gallant brutes, as e'er did draw;
Forby sax mae, I've sell't awa,   *beside six more,*
       That thou hast nurst: *sold*
They drew me thretteen pund an' twa,   *thirteen*
       The vera warst.   *worst*

Monie a sair daurk we twa hae wrought,   *hard day's labour*
An' wi' the weary warl' fought!   *world*
An' monie an' anxious day, I thought
       We wad be beat!
Yet here to *crazy Age* we're brought,   *infirm*
       Wi' something yet.

An' think na, my auld, trusty *Servan'*,
That now perhaps thou's less deservin,
An' thy *auld days* may end in starvin',   *old age*
       For my last fow,   *firlot*
A heapet *Stimpart*, I'll reserve ane   *measure of grain/*
       Laid by for you.   *quarter peck*

We've worn to crazy years thegither;   *lived*
We'll toyte about wi' ane anither;   *totter/walk like*
Wi' tentie care I'll flit thy tether,   *old age*
       To some hain'd rig,   *watchful, change*
Whare ye may nobly rax your leather,   *reserved field*
       Wi' sma' fatigue.   *stretch, skin*

The Cotter's Saturday Night
Inscribed to R. A****, Esq

Let not Ambition mock their useful toil,
  Their homely joys, and destiny obscure;
Nor Grandeur hear, with a disdainful smile,
  The short and simple annals of the Poor.
                                        Gray

I

My lov'd, my honor'd, much respected friend,
  No mercenary Bard his homage pays;
With honest pride, I scorn each selfish end,
  My dearest meed, a friend's esteem and   reward
    praise:
To you I sing, in simple Scottish lays,
  The lowly train in life's sequester'd scene;
The native feelings strong, the guileless ways,
  What A**** in a Cottage would have been;
Ah! tho' his worth unknown, far happier   believe
    there I ween!

II

                                                 blows, rushing
November chill blaws loud wi' angry sugh;   sound
  The short'ning winter-day is near a close;
The miry beasts retreating frae the pleugh;   plough
  The black'ning trains o' craws to their   crows
    repose:
The toil-worn COTTER frae his labor goes,   farm tenant/cottager
  This night his weekly moil is at an end,   drudgery
Collects his spades, his mattocks and his hoes,
  Hoping the morn in ease and rest to spend,

48

And weary, o'er the moor, his course does
   homeward bend.

III

At length his lonely Cot appears in view,   cottage
  Beneath the shelter of an aged tree,
The expectant *wee-things*, toddlan, stacher   stagger
   through
  To meet their *Dad*, wi' flichterin noise and   fluttering
   glee,
His wee-bit ingle, blinkan bonilie,   little bit of fire
  His clean hearth-stane, his thrifty *Wifie's* stone
   smile,
The *lisping infant*, prattling on his knee,
  Does a' his weary *kiaugh* and care beguile, 'carking anxiety' (B)
And makes him quite forget his labor and his
   toil.

IV

Belyve, the *elder bairns* come drapping in,   soon, dropping
  At *Service* out, amang the Farmers roun';
Some ca' the pleugh, some herd, some tentie drive, careful,
   run   run
  A cannie errand to a neebor town: quiet, neighbouring
Their eldest hope, their *Jenny*, woman-grown,
  In youthfu' bloom, Love sparkling in her e'e, eye
Comes hame, perhaps, to shew a braw new   good-looking
   gown,
  Or deposite her sair-won penny-fee,   hard-won
To help her *Parents* dear, if they in hardship
   be.

49

V

With joy unfeign'd, *brothers* and *sisters* meet,
  And each for other's weelfare kindly spiers: asks
The social hours, swift-wing'd, unnotic'd fleet;   news/uncommon
  Each tells the uncos that he sees or hears.   things
The Parents partial eye their hopeful years;
  Anticipation forward points the view;
The *Mother*, wi' her needle and her sheers,
  Gars auld claes look amaist as weel's the   makes, clothes
     new;
The *Father* mixes a' wi' admonition due.

VI

Their Master's and their Mistress's command,
  The *youngkers* a' are warned to obey;
And mind their labors wi' an eydent hand,   diligent
  And ne'er, tho' out of sight, to jauk or play: 'dally, trifle' (B)
'And O! be sure to fear the LORD alway!
  And mind your *duty*, duly, morn and night!
Lest in temptation's path ye gang astray,
  Implore his *counsel* and assisting *might*:
They nerve sought in vain that sought the
    LORD aright.'

VII

But hark! a rap comes gently to the door;
  Jenny, wha kens the meaning o' the same,
Tells how a neebor lad came o'er the moor,
  To do some errands, and convoy her hame.   escort
The wily Mother sees the *conscious flame*
  Sparkle in *Jenny's* e'e, and flush her cheek,
With heart-struck, anxious care enquires his
    name,

While Jenny hafflins is afraid to speak;   half
Weel-pleas'd the Mother hears, it's nae wild,
    worthless *Rake*.

VIII

With kindly welcome, *Jenny* brings him ben;
  A *strappan* youth; he takes the Mother's eye;
Blythe *Jenny* sees the *visit's* no ill taen;
  The Father cracks of horses, pleughs and kye.   talks, cattle
The *Youngster's* artless heart o'erflows wi' joy,
  But blate and laithfu', scarce can weel   shy, bashful
    behave;
The Mother, wi' a woman's wiles, can spy
  What makes the *youth* sae bashfu' and sae
    grave;
Weel-pleas'd to think her *bairn's* respected like
    the lave.   rest

IX

O happy love! where love like this is found!
  O heart-felt raptures! bliss beyond compare!
I've paced much this weary, *mortal round*,
  And sage EXPERIENCE bids me this declare –
'If Heaven a draught of heavenly pleasure
    spare,
  One *cordial* in this melancholy *Vale*,
'Tis when a youthful, loving, *modest* Pair,
  In other's arms, breathe out the tender tale,
Beneath the milk-white thorn that scents the
    ev'ning gale.'

X

Is there, in human form, that bears a heart –
  A Wretch! a Villain! lost to love and truth!
That can, with studied, sly, ensnaring art,
  Betray sweet Jenny's unsuspecting youth?
Curse on his perjur'd arts! dissembling
      smooth!
  Are Honor, Virtue, Conscience, all exil'd?
Is there no Pity, no relenting Ruth,
  Points to the Parents fondling o'er their
      Child?
Then paints the ruin'd Maid, and their distraction
      wild!

XI

But now the Supper crowns their simple
      board,
  The healsome Porritch, chief of SCOTIA's food: wholesome, porridge
The soupe their only Hawkie does afford,   drink, cow
  That 'yont the hallan snugly chows her cood: beyond, partition, chews, cud
The Dame brings forth, in complimental mood,
  To grace the lad, her weel-hain'd kebbuck,   -kept, cheese
      fell,   pungent
And aft he's prest, and aft he ca's it guid;
  The frugal Wifie, garrulous, will tell,
How 'twas a towmond auld, sin' Lint was i'   twelvemonth, flax flower
      the bell.

XII

The chearfu' Supper done, wi' serious face,
  They, round the ingle, form a circle wide;
The Sire turns o'er, with patriarchal grace,

The big *ha'-Bible*, ance his *Father's* pride: hall-
His bonnet rev'rently is laid aside,
  His *lyart haffets* wearing thin and bare;   grey, temples
Those strains that once did sweet in ZION
    glide,
He wales a portion with judicious care;   chooses
'And let us worship GOD*!'* he says with solemn
    air.

XIII

They chant their artless notes in simple guise;
  They tune their *hearts*, by far the noblest aim:
Perhaps *Dundee's* wild warbling measures rise,
  Or plaintive *Martyrs*, worthy of the name;
Or noble *Elgin* beets the heaven-ward flame,   'adds fuel to' (B)
  The sweetest far of SCOTIA's holy lays:
Compar'd with these, *Italian trills* are tame;
  The tickl'd ears no heart-felt raptures raise,
Nae unison hae they, with our CREATOR's
    praise.

XIV

The priest-like Father reads the sacred page,
  How *Abram* was the Friend of GOD on high;
Or, *Moses* bade eternal warfare wage,
  With *Amalek's* ungracious progeny;
Or how the *royal Bard* did groaning lye,
  Beneath the stroke of Heaven's avenging ire;
Or *Job's* pathetic plaint, and wailing cry,
  Or rapt *Isaiah's* wild, seraphic fire;
Or other *Holy Seers* that tune the *sacred lyre*.

XV

Perhaps the *Christian Volume* is the theme,
  How *guiltless blood* for guilty *man* was shed;
How HE, who bore in Heaven the second
      name,
  Had not on Earth whereon to lay His head:
How His first *followers* and *servants* sped;
  The *Precepts sage* they wrote to many a land:
How *he*, who lone in *Patmos* banished,
  Saw in the sun a mighty angel stand;
And heard great *Bab'lon's* doom pronounc'd by
      Heaven's command.

XVI

Then kneeling down to HEAVEN'S ETERNAL
      KING,
  The *Saint*, the *Father*, and the *Husband* prays:
Hope 'springs exulting on triumphant wing,'[1]
  That *thus* they all shall meet in future days:
There, ever bask in *uncreated rays*,
  No more to sigh, or shed the bitter tear,
Together hymning their CREATOR's praise,
  In *such society*, yet still more dear;
While circling Time moves round in an
      eternal sphere.

XVII

Compar'd with *this*, how poor Religion's
      pride,
  In all the pomp of *method*, and of *art*,

---

[1] Pope's *Windsor Forest*.

When men display to congregations wide,
  Devotion's ev'ry grace, except the *heart!*
The POWER, incens'd, the Pageant will desert,
  The pompous strain, the sacerdotal stole;
But haply, in some *Cottage* far apart,
  May hear, well pleas'd, the language
    of the *Soul*;
And in His *Book of Life* the Inmates poor enroll.

XVIII

Then homeward all take off their sev'ral way;
  The youngling *Cottagers* retire to rest:
The Parent-pair their *secret homage* pay,
  And proffer up to Heaven the warm request,
That HE who stills the *raven's* clam'rous nest,
  And decks the lily fair in flow'ry pride,
Would, in the way *His Wisdom* sees the best,
  For *them* and for their little *ones* provide;
But chiefly, in their hearts with *Grace divine*
    preside.

XIX

From scenes like these, old SCOTIA's grandeur
    springs,
  That makes her lov'd at home, rever'd
    abroad:
Princes and lords are but the breath of kings,
  'An honest man's the noblest work of GOD:'
And *certes*, in fair Virtue's heavenly road,
  The *Cottage* leaves the *Palace* far behind:
What is a lordling's pomp? a cumbrous load,
  Disguising oft the *wretch* of human kind,
Studied in arts of Hell, in wickedness refin'd!

XX

O SCOTIA! my dear, my native soil!
  For whom my warmest wish to Heaven is
      sent!
Long may thy hardy sons of rustic toil,
  Be blest with health, and peace, and sweet
      content!
And O may Heaven their simple lives prevent
  From Luxury's contagion, weak and vile!
Then howe'er crowns and coronets be rent,
  A virtuous Populace may rise the while,
And stand a wall of fire around their much-
      lov'd ISLE.

XXI

O THOU! who pour'd the patriotic tide,
  That stream'd thro' great, unhappy WALLACE'
      heart;
Who dar'd to, nobly, stem tyrannic pride,
  Or nobly die, the second glorious part:
(The Patriot's GOD, peculiarly thou art,
  His friend, inspirer, guardian and reward!)
O never, never SCOTIA's realm desert,
  But still the Patriot, and the Patriot-Bard,
In bright succession raise, her Ornament and
      Guard!

To A Mouse

On turning her up in her Nest, with the Plough, November, 1785

Wee, sleeket, cowran, tim'rous *beastie*,   sleek, fearful, little creature
O, what a panic's in thy breastie!   little breast
Thou need na start awa sae hasty,
         Wi' bickering brattle!   sound of scamper
I wad be laith to rin an' chase thee,   loath, run
         Wi' murd'ring *pattle*!   plough-staff

I'm truly sorry Man's dominion
Has broken Nature's social union,
An' justifies that ill opinion,
         Which makes thee startle,
At me, thy poor, earth-born companion,
         An' *fellow-mortal*!

I doubt na, whyles, but thou may *thieve*;
What then? poor beastie, thou maun live!
A *daimen-icker* in a *thrave*   occasional ear of corn, 24 sheaves
         'S a sma' request:
I'll get a blessin wi' the lave,   what's left/the rest
         An' never miss't!

Thy wee-bit *housie*, too, in ruin!
Its silly wa's the win's are strewin!   frail, winds
An' naething, now, to big a new ane,   build
         O' foggage green!   rank grass
An' bleak *December's winds* ensuin,
         Baith snell an' keen!   bitter

Thou saw the fields laid bare an' wast,   waste
An' weary *Winter* comin fast,
An' cozie here, beneath the blast,
       Thou thought to dwell,
Till crash! the cruel *coulter* past   iron cutter of
       Out thro' thy cell.   plough

That wee-bit heap o' leaves an' *stibble*,   stubble
Has cost thee monie a weary nibble!
Now thou's turn'd out, for a' thy trouble,
       But house or hald,   without refuge
To thole the Winter's *sleety dribble*,   endure
       An' *cranreuch* cauld!   hoar-frost

But Mousie, thou art no thy-lane,   not alone
In proving *foresight* may be vain:
The best laid schemes o' *Mice* an' *Men*,
       Gang aft agley,   awry
An' lea'e us nought but grief an' pain,
       For promis'd joy!

Still, thou art blest, compar'd wi' *me*!
The *present* only toucheth thee:
But Och! I *backward* cast my e'e,   eye
       On prospects drear!
An' *forward*, tho' I canna *see*,
       I *guess* an' *fear*!

To A Mountain-Daisy

On turning one down, with the Plough, in April —— 1786

Wee, modest, crimson-tipped flow'r,
Thou's met me in an evil hour;
For I maun crush amang the stoure   dust
      Thy slender stem:
To spare thee now is past my pow'r,
      Thou bonie gem.

Alas! it's no thy neebor sweet,   neighbour
The bonie *Lark*, companion meet!
Bending thee 'mang the dewy weet!   wet
      Wi's spreckl'd breast,
When upward-springing, blythe, to greet
      The purpling East.

Cauld blew the bitter-biting *North*
Upon thy early, humble birth;
Yet chearfully thou glinted forth
      Amid the storm,
Scarce rear'd above the *Parent-earth*
      Thy tender form.

The flaunting flow'rs our Gardens yield,
High-shelt'ring woods and wa's maun shield,
But thou, beneath the random bield   shelter
      O' clod or stane,   stone
Adorns the histie *stibble-field*,   bare, stubble-
      Unseen, alane.   alone

There, in thy scanty mantle clad,
Thy snawie bosom sun-ward spread,   snowy
Thou lifts thy unassuming head

59

In humble guise;
But now the *share* uptears thy bed,   ploughshare
        And low thou lies!

Such is the fate of artless Maid,
Sweet *flow'ret* of the rural shade!
By Love's simplicity betray'd,
        And guileless trust,
Till she, like thee, all soil'd, is laid
        Low i' the dust.

Such is the fate of simple Bard,
On Life's rough ocean luckless starr'd!
Unskilful he to note the card
        Of *prudent Lore*,
Till billows rage, and gales blow hard,
        And whelm him o'er!

Such fate to *suffering worth* is giv'n,
Who long with wants and woes has striv'n,
By human pride or cunning driv'n
        To Mis'ry's brink,
Till wrench'd of ev'ry stay but HEAV'N,
        He, ruin'd, sink!

Ev'n thou who mourn'st the *Daisy's* fate,
That fate is thine – no distant date;
Stern Ruin's *plough-share* drives, elate,
        Full on thy bloom,
Till crush'd beneath the *furrow's* weight,
        Shall be thy doom!

Epistle To A Young Friend
May —— 1786

I

I Lang hae thought, my youthfu' friend,
  A Something to have sent you,
Tho' it should serve nae other end
  Than just a kind memento;
But how the subject theme may gang,
  Let time and chance determine,
Perhaps it may turn out a Sang;
  Perhaps, turn out a Sermon.

II

Ye'll try the world soon my lad,
  And ANDREW dear believe me,
Ye'll find mankind an unco squad,
  And muckle they may grieve ye:
For care and trouble set your thought,
  Ev'n when your end's attained;
And a' your views may come to nought,
  Where ev'ry nerve is strained.

III

I'll no say, men are villains a';
  The real, harden'd wicked,
Whae hae nae check but *human law*,
  Are to a few restricked:
But Och, mankind are unco weak,
  An' little to be trusted;
If *Self* the wavering balance shake,
  It's rarely right adjusted!

IV

Yet they wha fa' in Fortune's strife,
  Their fate we should na censure,
For still th'important end of life,
  They equally may answer:
A man may hae an honest heart,
  Tho' Poortith hourly stare him;   poverty
A man may tak a neebor's part,   neighbour's
  Yet hae nae cash to spare him.

V

Ay free, aff han', your story tell,   offhand
  When wi' a bosom crony;
But still keep something to yoursel
  Ye scarcely tell to ony.
Conceal yoursel as weel's ye can
  Frae critical dissection;
But keek thro' ev'ry other man,   look/pry
  Wi' sharpen'd, sly inspection.

VI

The sacred lowe o' weel plac'd love,   flame
  Luxuriantly indulge it;
But never tempt th'illicit rove,   attempt
  Tho' naething should divulge it:
I waive the quantum o' the sin;   amount
  The hazard of concealing;
But Och! it hardens a' within,
  And petrifies the feeling!

VII

To catch Dame Fortune's golden smile,
  Assiduous wait upon her;
And gather gear by ev'ry wile,   money/property
  That's justify'd by Honor:
Not for to hide it in a *hedge*,
  Nor for a *train-attendant*;
But for the glorious priviledge
  Of being *independant*.

VIII

The fear o' Hell's a hangman's whip,
  To haud the wretch in order;   hold
But where ye feel your *Honor* grip,
  Let that ay be your border:
Its slightest touches, instant pause –
  Debar a' side-pretences;
And resolutely keep its laws,
  Uncaring consequences.

IX

The great CREATOR to revere,
  Must sure become the *Creature*;
But still the preaching cant forbear,
  And ev'n the rigid feature:
Yet ne'er with Wits prophane to range,
  Be complaisance extended;
An *atheist-laugh's* a poor exchange
  For *Deity offended*!

X

When ranting round in Pleasure's ring,   *frolicking*
  Religion may be blinded;
Or if she gie a *random-fling*,
  It may be little minded;
But when on Life we're tempest-driven,
  A Conscience but a canker –
A correspondence fix'd wi' Heav'n,
  Is sure a noble *anchor*!

XI

Adieu, dear, amiable Youth!
  Your *heart* can ne'er be wanting!
May Prudence, Fortitude and Truth
  Erect your brow undaunting!
In *ploughman phrase* 'GOD send you speed,'
  Still daily to grow wiser;
And may ye better reck the *rede*,   *heed the advice*
  Than ever did th'*Adviser*!

On a Scotch Bard gone to the West Indies

A' ye wha live by sowps o' drink,	mouthfuls
A' ye wha live by crambo-clink,	rhyme
A' ye wha live and never think,	
Come, mourn wi' me!	
Our billie's gien us a' a jink,	comrade, slip
An' owre the Sea.	

Lament him a' ye rantan core,	merry company
Wha dearly like a random-splore;	frolic
Nae mair he'll join the merry roar,	
In social key;	
For now he's taen anither shore,	
An' owre the Sea!	

The bonie lasses weel may wiss him,	wish
And in their dear petitions place him:	
The widows, wives, an' a' may bless him,	
Wi' tearfu' e'e;	eye
For weel I wat they'll sairly miss him	know
That's owre the Sea!	

O Fortune, they hae room to grumble!	
Hadst thou taen aff some drowsy bummle,	bungler
Wha can do nought but fyke an' fumble,	fuss
'Twad been nae plea;	
But he was gleg as onie wumble,	nimble, gimlet
That's owre the Sea!	

Auld, cantie KYLE may weepers wear,	cheerful
An' stain them wi' the saut, saut tear:	salt
'Twill mak her poor, auld heart, I fear,	
In flinders flee:	fragments

He was her *Laureat* monie a year,
    That's owre the Sea!

He saw Misfortune's cauld *Nor-west*
Lang-mustering up a bitter blast;
A Jillet brak his heart at last,   jilt
    Ill may she be!
So, took a birth afore the mast,   berth
    An' owre the Sea,

To tremble under Fortune's cummock;   cudgel
On scarce a bellyfu' o' *drummock*,   meal and water
Wi' his proud, independant stomach,
    Could ill agree;
So, row't his hurdies in a *hammock*,   rolled, buttocks
    An' owre the Sea.

He ne'er was gien to great misguidin,
Yet coin his pouches wad na bide in;   pockets
Wi' him it ne'er was *under hidin*;
    He dealt it free:
The *Muse* was a' that he took pride in,
    That's owre the Sea.

Jamaica bodies, use him weel,
An' hap him in a cozie biel: wrap, shelter
Ye'll find him ay a dainty chiel,   pleasant fellow
    An' fou o' glee: full
He wad na wrang'd the vera *Diel*,   wronged, very, Devil
    That's owre the Sea.

Fareweel, my *rhyme-composing billie*!   fellow
Your native soil was right ill-willie;   unkind
But may ye flourish like a lily,

Now bonilie!
I'll toast you in my hindmost *gillie*,   last gill
Tho' owre the Sea!

To A Louse
On Seeing one on a Lady's Bonnet at Church

Ha! whare ye gaun, ye crowlan ferlie!	crawling wonder
Your impudence protects you sairly:	indeed
I canna say but ye strunt rarely,	strut
Owre *gawze* and *lace*;	
Tho' faith, I fear ye dine but sparely,	
On sic a place.	

Ye ugly, creepan, blastet wonner,	wonder
Detested, shunn'd, by saunt an' sinner,	saint
How daur ye set your fit upon her,	dare, foot
Sae fine a *Lady*!	
Gae somewhere else and seek your dinner,	
On some poor body.	

Swith, in some beggar's haffet squattle;	off!, temple, squat
There ye may creep, and sprawl, and sprattle,	scramble
Wi' ither kindred, jumping cattle,	beasts
In shoals and nations;	families, tribes
Whare *horn* nor *bane* ne'er daur unsettle,	horn, bone
Your thick plantations.	

Now haud you there, ye're out of sight,	keep
Below the fatt'rels, snug and tight,	falderals
Na faith ye yet! ye'll no be right,	
Till ye've got on it,	
The vera tapmost, towrin height	very topmost
O' *Miss's bonnet*.	

My sooth! right bauld ye set your nose out,   bold
As plump an' gray as onie grozet: gooseberry
O for some rank, mercurial rozet,   resin
          Or fell, red smeddum,   deadly, powder
I'd gie you sic a hearty dose o't,
          Wad dress your droddum!   thrash, backside

I wad na been surpriz'd to spy
You on an auld wife's *flainen toy*;   flannel cap
Or aiblins some bit duddie boy,   perhaps, small
                                                         ragged
          On's *wylecoat*;   flannel vest
But Miss's fine *Lunardi*, fye!   balloon bonnet
          How daur ye do't?

O *Jenny* dinna toss your head,   do not
An' set your beauties a' abroad!   abroad
Ye little ken what cursed speed
          The blastie's makin!   ill-disposed creature
Thae *winks* and *finger-ends*, I dread,   those
          Are notice takin!

O wad some Pow'r the giftie gie us   little gift
To see oursels as others see us!
It wad frae monie a blunder free us
          An' foolish notion:
What airs in dress an' gait wad lea'e us
          And ev'n Devotion!

Epistle to J. L*****k

An Old Scotch Bard

April 1st, 1785

While briers an' woodbines budding green,   partridges,
An' Paitricks scraichan loud at e'en,   screaming, evening
And morning Poossie whiddan seen,   hare, scudding
       Inspire my Muse,
This freedom, in an unknown frien',
       I pray excuse.

On Fasteneen we had a rockin,   Shrove Tuesday,
To ca' the crack and weave our stockin;   spinning party
And there was muckle fun and jokin,   have a chat
       Ye need na doubt;
At length we had a hearty yokin,   set-to
       At *sang* about.   singing in turn

There was ae *sang*, amang the rest,
Aboon them a' it pleas'd me best,   above
That some kind husband had addrest,
       To some sweet wife:
It thirl'd the heart-strings thro' the breast,   thrilled
       A' to the life.

I've scarce heard ought describ'd sae weel,
What gen'rous, manly bosoms feel;
Thought I, 'Can this be *Pope*, or *Steele*,
       Or *Beattie's* wark;'   work
They tale me 'twas an odd kind chiel   told, fellow
       About Muirkirk.

70

It pat me fidgean-fain to hear't,   put, tingling / with pleasure
An' sae about him there I spier't;   asked
Then a' that kent him round declar'd,
         He had ingine,   wit
That name excell'd it, few cam near't,
         It was sae fine.

That set him to a pint of ale,
An' either douse or merry tale,   sober
Or rhymes an' sangs he'd made himsel,
         Or witty catches,
'Tween Inverness and Teviotdale,
         He had few matches.

Then up I gat, an swoor an aith,   swore, oath
Tho' I should pawn my pleugh an' graith,   plough, harness
Or die a cadger pownie's death,   hawker pony's
         At some dyke-back,   behind a wall
A pint an' gill I'd gie them baith,
         To hear your crack.   talk

But first an' foremost, I should tell,
Amaist as soon as I could spell,
I to the crambo-jingle fell,   rhyming
         Tho' rude an' rough,
Yet crooning to a body's sel,   humming, to oneself
         Does weel eneugh.   enough

I am nae Poet, in a sense,
But just a Rhymer like by chance,
An' hae to Learning nae pretence,
         Yet, what the matter?
Whene'er my Muse does on me glance,
         I jingle at her.

Your Critic-folk may cock their nose,
And say, 'How can you e'er propose,
You wha ken hardly *verse* frae *prose*,
   To mak a *sang*?'
But by your leaves, my learned foes,
   Ye're maybe wrang.   wrong

What's a' your jargon o' your Schools,
Your Latin names for horns an' stools;
If honest Nature made you *fools*,
   What sairs your Grammars?   serves
Ye'd better taen up *spades* and *shools*,   shovels
   Or *knappin-hammers*.   stone-breaking

A set o' dull, conceited Hashes,
Confuse their brains in *Colledge-classes*!
They *gang* in Stirks, and *come out* Asses,   steers/young
   Plain truth to speak;   bullocks
An' syne they think to climb Parnassus   then
   By dint o' Greek!

Gie me ae spark o' Nature's fire,
That's a' the learning I desire;
Then tho' I drudge thro' dub an' mire   puddle
   At pleugh or cart,
My Muse, tho' hamely in attire,
   May touch the heart.

O for a spunk o' ALLAN's glee,   spark
Or FERGUSSON's, the bauld an' slee,   bold, clever
Or bright L*****K's, my friend to be,
   If I can hit it!
That would be *lear* eneugh for me,   learning
   If I could get it.

72

Now, Sir, if ye hae friends enow,   enough
Tho' *real friends* I b'lieve are few,
Yet, if your catalogue be fow,   full
     I'se no insist;   I'll
But gif ye want ae friend that's true,   if
     I'm on your list.

I winna blaw about *mysel*,   will not brag
As ill I like my fauts to tell;   faults
But friends an' folk that wish me well,
     They sometimes roose me;   praise
Tho' I maun own, as monie still,
     As far abuse me.

There's ae *wee faut* they whiles lay to me,
I like the lasses – Gude forgie me!   God forgive
For monie a Plack they wheedle frae me,   coin
     At dance or fair:
Maybe some *ither thing* they gie me
     They weel can spare.

But MAUCHLINE Race or MAUCHLINE Fair,
I should be proud to meet you there;
We'se gie ae night's discharge to *care*,   we'll
     If we forgather,
An' hae a swap o' *rhymin-ware*,
     Wi' ane anither.

The *four-gill chap*, we'se gar him clatter,   cup, we'll make
An' kirs'n him wi' reekin water;   christen, steaming
Syne we'll sit down an' tak our whitter,   draught
     To chear our heart;
An' faith, we'se be *acquainted* better
     Before we part.

Awa ye selfish, warly race,   worldly
Wha think that havins, sense an' grace,   manners
Ev'n love an' friendship should give place
          To catch-the-plack!   coining money
I dinna like to see your face,   do not
          Nor hear your crack.

But ye whom social pleasure charms,
Whose hearts the tide of kindness warms,
Who hold your being on the terms,
          'Each aids the others,'
Come to my bowl, come to my arms,
          My friends, my brothers!

But to conclude my lang epistle,
As my auld pen's worn to the grissle;
Twa lines frae you wad gar me fissle,   make, tingle
          Who am, most fervent,
While I can either sing, or whissle,
          Your friend and servant.

Song

Tune, Corn rigs are bonie

I

It was upon a Lammas night,
　　When corn rigs are bonie,　　　　　ridges
Beneath the moon's unclouded light,
　　I held awa to Annie:　　　　　took my way
The time flew by, wi' tentless heed,　　careless
　　Till 'tween the late and early;
Wi' sma' persuasion she agreed,
　　To see me thro' the barley.

II

The sky was blue, the wind was still,
　　The moon was shining clearly;
I set her down, wi' right good will,
　　Amang the rigs o' barley:
I ken't her heart was a' my ain;　　　own
　　I lov'd her most sincerely;
I kiss'd her owre and owre again,
　　Amang the rigs o' barley.

III

I lock'd her in my fond embrace;
　　Her heart was beating rarely:
My blessings on that happy place,
　　Amang the rigs o' barley!
But by the moon and stars so bright,
　　That shone that night so clearly!
She ay shall bless that happy night,
　　Amang the rigs o' barley.

IV

I hae been blythe wi' Comrades dear;
   I hae been merry drinking;
I hae been joyfu' gath'rin gear;   money/property
   I hae been happy thinking;
But a' the pleasures e'er I saw,
   Tho' three times doubl'd fairly,
That happy night was worth them a',
   Amang the rigs o' barley.

CHORUS

Corn rigs, an' barley rigs,
   An' corn rigs are bonie:
I'll ne'er forget that happy night,
   Amang the rigs wi' Annie.

Song

Composed in *August*
Tune, *I had a horse, I had nae mair*

I

Now westlin winds, and slaught'ring guns   westerly
  Bring Autumn's pleasant weather;
And the moorcock springs, on whirring
    wings,
  Amang the blooming heather:
Now waving grain, wide o'er the plain,
  Delights the weary Farmer;
And the moon shines bright, when I rove at
    night,
  To muse upon my Charmer.

II

The Partridge loves the fruitful fells;
  The Plover loves the mountains;
The Woodcock haunts the lonely dells;
  The soaring Hern the fountains:
Thro' lofty groves, the Cushat roves,   wood-pigeon
  The path of man to shun it;
The hazel bush o'erhangs the Thrush,
  The spreading thorn the Linnet.

III

Thus ev'ry kind their pleasure find,
  The savage and the tender;
Some social join, and leagues combine;
  Some solitary wander:
Avaunt, away! the cruel sway,

Tyrannic man's dominion;
The Sportsman's joy, the murd'ring cry,
  The flutt'ring, gory pinion!

IV

But PEGGY dear, the ev'ning's clear,
  Thick flies the skimming Swallow;
The sky is blue, the fields in view,
  All fading-green and yellow:
Come let us stray our gladsome way,
  And view the charms of Nature;
The rustling corn, the fruited thorn,
  And ev'ry happy creature.

V

We'll gently walk, and sweetly talk,
  Till the silent moon shine clearly;
I'll grasp thy waist, and fondly prest,
  Swear how I love thee dearly:
Not vernal show'rs to budding flow'rs,
  Not Autumn to the Farmer,
So dear can be, as thou to me,
  My fair, my lovely Charmer!

A Bard's Epitaph

Is there a whim-inspir'd fool,
Owre fast for thought, owre hot for rule,   too
Owre blate to seek, owre proud to snool,   diffident, submit
     Let him draw near;   tamely
And o'er this grassy heap sing dool,   lament
     And drap a tear.   drop

Is there a Bard of rustic song,
Who, noteless, steals the crouds among,
That weekly this area throng,   churchyard
     O, pass not by!
But with a frater-feeling strong,   brother
     Here, heave a sigh.

Is there a man whose judgment clear,
Can others teach the course to steer,
Yet runs, himself, life's mad career,
     Wild as the wave,
Here pause – and thro' the starting tear,
     Survey this grave.

The poor Inhabitant below
Was quick to learn and wise to know,
And keenly felt the friendly glow,
     And *softer flame*;
But thoughtless follies laid him low,
     And stain'd his name!

Reader attend – whether thy soul
Soars fancy's flights beyond the pole,
Or darkling grubs this earthly hole,
     In low pursuit,
Know, prudent, cautious, *self-controul*
     Is Wisdom's root.

79

Holy Willie's Prayer

And send the Godly in a pet to pray —
Pope

ARGUMENT

Holy Willie was a rather oldish batchelor Elder in the parish of Mauchline, and much and justly famed for that polemical chattering which ends in tippling Orthodoxy, and for that Spiritualized Bawdry which refines to Liquorish Devotion. — In a Sessional process with a gentleman in Mauchline, a Mr Gavin Hamilton, Holy Willie, and his priest, father Auld, after full hearing in the Presbytery of Ayr, came off but second best; owing partly to the oratorical powers of Mr Robt Aiken, Mr Hamilton's Counsel; but chiefly to Mr Hamilton's being one of the most irreproachable and truly respectable characters in the country. — On losing his Process, the Muse overheard him at his devotions as follows —

O Thou that in the heavens does dwell!
Wha, as it pleases best thysel,
Sends ane to heaven and ten to h-ll,
  A' for thy glory!
And no for ony gude or ill
  They've done before thee. —

I bless and praise thy matchless might,
When thousands thou has left in night,
That I am here before thy sight,
  For gifts and grace,
A burning and a shining light
  To a' this place. —

What was I, or my generation,
That I should get such exaltation?
I, wha deserv'd most just damnation,
        For broken laws
Sax thousand years ere my creation,
        Thro' Adam's cause!

When from my mother's womb I fell,
Thou might hae plunged me deep in hell,
To gnash my gooms, and weep, and wail,   gums
        In burning lakes,
Where damned devils roar and yell
        Chain'd to their stakes. –

Yet I am here, a chosen sample,
To shew thy grace is great and ample:
I'm here, a pillar o' thy temple
        Strong as a rock,
A guide, a ruler and example
        To a' thy flock. –

[O L—d thou kens what zeal I bear,
When drinkers drink, and swearers swear,
And singin' there, and dancin' here,
        Wi' great an' sma';
For I am keepet by thy fear,
        Free frae them a'. –]

But yet – O L—d – confess I must –
At times I'm fash'd wi' fleshly lust;   afflicted
And sometimes too, in warldly trust
        Vile Self gets in;
But thou remembers we are dust,
        Defil'd wi' sin. –

O L—d – yestreen – thou kens – wi' Meg –
Thy pardon I sincerely beg!
O may't ne'er be a living plague,
        To my dishonor!
And I'll ne'er lift a lawless leg
        Again upon her. –

Besides, I farther maun avow,   must
Wi' Leezie's lass, three times – I trow –
But L—d, that friday I was fou   drunk
        When I cam near her;
Or else, thou kens, thy servant true
        Wad never steer her. –

Maybe thou lets this fleshly thorn
Buffet thy servant e'en and morn,
Lest he o'er proud and high should turn,
        That he's sae gifted;
If sae, thy hand maun e'en be borne
        Untill thou lift it. –

L—d bless thy Chosen in this place,
For here thou has a chosen race:
But G—d, confound their stubborn face,
        And blast their name,
Wha bring thy rulers to disgrace
        And open shame. –

L—d mind Gaun Hamilton's deserts!
He drinks, and swears, and plays at cartes,   cards
Yet has sae mony taking arts
        Wi' Great and Sma',
Frae G—d's ain priest the people's hearts
        He steals awa. –

And when we chasten'd him therefore,
Thou kens how he bred sic a splore,   uproar
And set the warld in a roar
     O' laughin at us:
Curse thou his basket and his store,
     Kail and potatoes. –   cabbage

L—d hear my earnest cry and prayer
Against that Presbytry of Ayr!
Thy strong right hand, L—d, make it bare
     Upon their heads!
L—d visit them, and dinna spare,
     For their misdeeds!

O L—d my G-d, that glib-tongu'd Aiken!
My very heart and flesh are quaking
To think how I sat, sweating, shaking,
     And p-ss'd wi' dread,
While Auld wi' hingin lip gaed sneaking
     And hid his head!

L—d, in thy day o' vengeance try him!
L—d visit him that did employ him!
And pass not in thy mercy by them,
     Nor hear their prayer;
But for thy people's sake destroy them,
     And dinna spare!

But L—d, remember me and mine
Wi' mercies temporal and divine!
That I for grace and gear may shine,
     Excell'd by nane!
And a' the glory shall be thine!
     AMEN! AMEN!

Tam o' Shanter. A Tale

Of Brownyis and of Bogillis full is this buke.
                                    Gawin Douglas

When chapman billies leave the street,	pedlar lads
And drouthy neebors, neebors meet,	thirsty neighbours
As market-days are wearing late,	
An' folk begin to tak the gate;	take the road
While we sit bousing at the nappy,	boozing, ale
And getting fou and unco happy,	drunk
We think na on the lang Scots miles,	
The mosses, waters, slaps, and styles,	gaps in walls
That lie between us and our hame,	
Whare sits our sulky sullen dame,	
Gathering her brows like gathering storm,	
Nursing her wrath to keep it warm.	

This truth fand honest *Tam o' Shanter*,	found
As he frae Ayr ae night did canter,	
(Auld Ayr, wham ne'er a town surpasses,	old
For honest men and bonny lasses.)	

O *Tam*! hadst thou but been sae wise,	
As ta'en thy ain wife *Kate's* advice!	own
She tauld thee weel thou was a skellum,	told, well, rascal
A blethering, blustering, drunken blellum;	babbler
That frae November till October,	
Ae market-day thou was nae sober;	
That ilka melder, wi' the miller,	time for corn-grinding
Thou sat as lang as thou had siller;	silver
That every naig was ca'd a shoe on;	[time a] pony was shod
The smith and thee gat roaring fou on;	
That at the L—d's house, even on Sunday,	

84

Thou drank wi' Kirkton Jean till Monday.
She prophesied that late or soon,
Thou would be found deep drown'd in Doon;
Or catch'd wi' warlocks in the mirk,   caught, darkness
By *Alloway's* auld haunted kirk.

Ah, gentle dames! it gars me greet,   makes, weep
To think how mony counsels sweet,
How mony lengthen'd sage advices,
The husband frae the wife despises!

But to our tale: Ae market-night,
Tam had got planted unco right;   just
Fast by an ingle, bleezing finely,   fireside, blazing
Wi' reaming swats, that drank divinely;   foaming beer
And at his elbow, Souter *Johnny*,   Shoemaker
His ancient, trusty, drouthy crony;
Tam lo'ed him like a vera brither;   loved, real brother
They had been fou for weeks thegither.   together
The night drave on wi' sangs and clatter;   drove, gossip
And ay the ale was growing better:
The landlady and *Tam* grew gracious,
Wi' favours, secret, sweet, and precious:
The Souter tauld his queerest stories;   told
The landlord's laugh was ready chorus:
The storm without might rair and rustle,   roar
Tam did na mind the storm a whistle.

Care, mad to see a man sae happy,
E'en drown'd himsel amang the nappy: even
As bees flee hame wi' lades o' treasure,   fly, loads
The minutes wing'd their way wi' pleasure:
Kings may be blest, but *Tam* was glorious,
O'er a' the ills o' life victorious!

85

But pleasures are like poppies spread,
You seize the flower, its bloom is shed;
Or like the snow falls in the river,
A moment white – then melts for ever;
Or like the borealis race,
That flit ere you can point their place;
Or like the rainbow's lovely form
Evanishing amid the storm. –
Nae man can tether time or tide;
The hour approaches *Tam* maun ride;
That hour, o' night's black arch the key-stane,   -stone
That dreary hour he mounts his beast in;
And sic a night he taks the road in,
As ne'er poor sinner was abroad in.

The wind blew as 'twad blawn its last;   if blowing
The rattling showers rose on the blast;
The speedy gleams the darkness swallow'd;
Loud, deep, and lang, the thunder bellow'd:
That night, a child might understand,
The Deil had business on his hand.   Devil

Weel mounted on his gray mare, *Meg*,
A better never lifted leg,
Tam skelpit on thro' dub and mire,   hurried, mud
Despising wind, and rain, and fire;
Whiles holding fast his gude blue bonnet;
Whiles crooning o'er some auld Scots sonnet;
Whiles glowring round wi' prudent cares,
Lest bogles catch him unawares: spectres/goblins
Kirk-Alloway was drawing nigh,
Whare ghaists and houlets nightly cry. –   ghosts, owls

By this time he was cross the ford,
Whare, in the snaw, the chapman smoor'd;   snow, smothered
And past the birks and meikle stane,   birches, stone
Whare drunken *Charlie* brak's neck-bane;   broke, -bone
And thro' the whins, and by the cairn,
Whare hunters fand the murder'd bairn;   child
And near the thorn, aboon the well,   above
Whare *Mungo's* mither hang'd hersel. –   mother
  Before him *Doon* pours all his floods;
The doubling storm roars thro' the woods;
The lightnings flash from pole to pole;
Near and more near the thunders roll:
When, glimmering thro' the groaning trees,
Kirk-Alloway seem'd in a bleeze;
Thro' ilka bore the beams were glancing;   crevice
And loud resounded mirth and dancing. –

  Inspiring bold *John Barleycorn!*
What dangers thou canst make us scorn!
Wi' tippeny, we fear nae evil;   ale at 2d a pint
Wi' usquabae, we'll face the devil! –   whisky
The swats sae ream'd in *Tammie's* noddle,   head
Fair play, he car'd na deils a boddle.   worthless coin
But *Maggie* stood right sair astonish'd,   sore
Till, by the heel and hand admonish'd,
She ventured forward on the light;
And, vow! *Tam* saw an unco sight!
Warlocks and witches in a dance;
Nae cotillion brent new frae France,   brand
But hornpipes, jigs, strathspeys, and reels,
Put life and mettle in their heels.
A winnock-bunker in the east,   window-seat
There sat auld Nick, in shape o' beast;   The Devil
A towzie tyke, black, grim, and large,   ragged mongrel

87

To gie them music was his charge: give
He screw'd the pipes, and gart them skirl,   made shriek
Till roof and rafters a' did dirl. —   shake
Coffins stood round, like open presses,   cupboards
That shaw'd the dead in their last dresses;   showed
And by some devilish cantraip slight   magic/trick
Each in its cauld hand held a light. —   cold
By which heroic *Tam* was able
To note upon the haly table,   holy
A murderer's banes in gibbet-airns;   bones, -irons
Twa span-lang, wee, unchristen'd bairns;   nine-inch, small
A thief, new-cutted frae a rape,   rope
Wi' his last gasp his gab did gape;   mouth
Five tomahawks, wi' blude red-rusted;   blood
Five scimitars, wi' murder crusted;
A garter, which a babe had strangled;
A knife, a father's throat had mangled,
Whom his ain son o' life bereft,
The grey hairs yet stack to the heft;   stuck
Wi' mair o' horrible and awefu',
Which even to name wad be unlawfu'.

  As *Tammie* glowr'd, amazed, and curious,
The mirth and fun grew fast and furious:
The piper loud and louder blew
The dancers quick and quicker flew;
They reel'd, they set, they cross'd, they   linked arms
    cleekit,   witch, sweated,
Till ilka carlin swat and reekit,   reeked
And coost her duddies to the wark,   cast, rags, work
And linket at it in her sark!   shift

  Now, *Tam*, O *Tam*! had thae been queans,   young girls
A' plump and strapping in their teens,
Their sarks, instead o' creeshie flannen,   greasy flannel

88

Been snaw-white seventeen hunder linnen!   best linen
Thir breeks o' mine, my only pair,   these trousers
That ance were plush, o' gude blue hair,
I wad hae gi'en them off my hurdies,   buttocks
For ae blink o' the bonie burdies!   moment, girls

  But wither'd beldams, auld and droll,
Rigwoodie hags wad spean a foal,   withered, wean
Lowping and flinging on a crummock,   jumping, crook
I wonder didna turn thy stomach.

  But Tam kend what was what fu' brawlie,   full well
There was ae winsome wench and wawlie,   good-looking
That night enlisted in the core,
(Lang after kend on Carrick shore;
For mony a beast to dead she shot,
And perish'd mony a bony boat,
And shook baith meikle corn and bear,   both, barley
And kept the country-side in fear:)
Her cutty sark, o' Paisley harn,   short, linen
That while a lassie she had worn,   girl
In longitude tho' sorely scanty,
It was her best, and she was vauntie. –   vain/proud
Ah! little kend thy reverend grannie,
That sark she coft for her wee Nannie,   bought
Wi' twa pund Scots, ('twas a' her riches),   two pounds
Wad ever grac'd a dance of witches!   would have

  But here my Muse her wing maun cour;   cower
Sic flights are far beyond her pow'r;
To sing how Nannie lap and flang,   leapt, kicked
(A souple jade she was, and strang),   supple wench
And how Tam stood, like ane bewitch'd,
And thought his very een enrich'd;   eyes

89

Even Satan glowr'd, and fidg'd fu' fain,   *twitched with excitement*
And hotch'd and blew wi' might and main: *fidgeted*
Till first ae caper, syne anither,   *then*
Tam tint his reason a' thegither,   *lost*
And roars out, 'Weel done, Cutty-sark!'
And in an instant all was dark:
And scarcely had he Maggie rallied,
When out the hellish legion sallied.

As bees bizz out wi' angry fyke,   *buzz, commotion*
When plundering herds assail their byke;   *hive*
As open pussie's mortal foes,
When, pop! she starts before their nose;
As eager runs the market-crowd,
When 'Catch the thief!' resounds aloud;
So Maggie runs, the witches follow,
Wi' mony an eldritch skreech and hollow.   *unearthly shriek*

Ah, Tam! Ah, Tam! thou'll get thy fairin!   *just reward*
In hell they'll roast thee like a herrin!
In vain thy Kate awaits thy comin!
Kate soon will be a woefu' woman!
Now, do thy speedy utmost, Meg,
And win the key-stane[1] of the brig;   *bridge*
There at them thou thy tail may toss,
A running stream they dare na cross.
But ere the key-stane she could make,
The fient a tail she had to shake!   *Never a*
For Nannie, far before the rest,

[1] It is a well known fact that witches, or any evil spirits, have no power to follow a poor wight any farther than the middle of the next running stream. – It may be proper likewise to mention to the benighted traveller, that when he falls in with *bogles*, whatever danger may be in his going forward, there is much more hazard in turning back.

Hard upon noble Maggie prest,
And flew at *Tam* wi' furious ettle;   aim
But little wist she Maggie's mettle —
Ae spring brought off her master hale,   completely
But left behind her ain grey tail:
The carlin caught her by the rump,
And left poor Maggie scarce a stump.

  Now, wha this tale o' truth shall read,
Ilk man and mother's son, take heed:
Whene'er to drink you are inclin'd,
Or cutty-sarks run in your mind,
Think, ye may buy the joys o'er dear,
Remember Tam o' Shanter's mare.

To A Haggis

Fair fa' your honest, sonsie face,	plump
Great Chieftan o' the Puddin-race!	Pudding
Aboon them a' ye tak your place,	above
Painch, tripe, or thairm:	stomach, intestines
Weel are ye wordy o' a grace	well worthy
As lang's my arm.	long

The groaning trencher there ye fill,	
Your hurdies like a distant hill,	buttocks
Your pin wad help to mend a mill	skewer
In time o' need,	
While thro' your pores the dews distil	
Like amber bead.	drop of whisky

His knife see Rustic-labour dight,	wipe
An' cut you up wi' ready slight,	
Teaching your gushing entrails bright	
Like onie ditch;	any
And then, O what a glorious sight,	
Warm-reekin, rich!	-steaming

Then, horn for horn they stretch an' strive,	spoon
Deil tak the hindmost, on they drive,	devil take the last
Till a' their weel-swall'd kytes belyve	all well-swollen bellies, soon
Are bent like drums;	
Then auld Guidman, maist like to rive,	master, almost fit to burst
Bethankit hums.	hums the Grace

Is there that owre his French ragout,	over
Or olio that wad staw a sow,	oil would satiate
Or fricassee wad mak her spew	make
Wi' perfect sconner,	disgust

Looks down wi' sneering, scornfu' view
           On sic a dinner?   *such*

Poor devil! See him owre his trash,
As feckless as a' wither'd rash,   *weak, withered rush*
His spindle shank a guid whip-lash,   *skinny leg, good*
           His nieve a nit;   *fist, nut*
Thro' bluidy flood or field to dash,
           O how unfit!

But mark the Rustic, *haggis-fed*,
The trembling earth resounds his tread,
Clap in his walie nieve a blade,   *ample fist*
           He'll mak it whissle;   *make whistle*
An' legs, an' arms, an' heads will sned,   *trim*
           Like taps o' thrissle.   *tops, thistle*

Ye Pow'rs wha mak mankind your care,
And dish them out their bill o' fare,
Auld Scotland wants nae stinkin ware   *watery*
           That jaups in luggies;   *spills, little bowls*
                                              with handles
But, if ye wish her gratefu' pray'r,
           Gie her a *haggis*!   *give*

Death and Doctor Hornbook. *A True Story*

Some books are lies frae end to end,
And some great lies were never penn'd;
Ev'n Ministers they hae been kenn'd,   known
      In holy rapture,
Great lies and nonsense baith to vend,   both
      And nail't wi' Scripture.

But this that I am gaun to tell,   going
Which lately on a night befel,
Is just as true's the Deil's in h-ll,
      Or Dublin city:
That e'er he nearer comes oursel
      'S a muckle pity,   great

The Clachan yill had made me canty,   village ale
I was na fou, but just had plenty;   drunk
I stacher'd whyles, but ye took tent ay   staggered at times, care
      To free the ditches;
An' hillocks, stanes, an' bushes kenn'd ay   always
      Frae ghaists an' witches.   ghosts

The rising moon began to glowr
The distant *Cumnock* hills out-owre;   over
To count her horns, wi' a' my pow'r,
      I set mysel;
But whether she had three or four,
      I cou'd na tell.   could not

I was come round about the hill,
And todlin down on *Willie's* mill,   tottering
Setting my staff wi' a' my skill,
      To keep me sicker;   sure

Tho' leeward whyles, against my will,
              I took a bicker.   *stagger*

I there wi' *Something* does forgather,
That pat me in an eerie swither;   *put, doubt*
An awfu' scythe, out-owre ae shouther,   *one shoulder*
              Clear-dangling, hang;
A three-tae'd leister on the ither   *toed, trident, other*

              Lay, large an' lang.

Its stature seem'd lang Scotch ells twa,   *roughly a yard long*
The queerest shape that e'er I saw,
For fient a wame it had ava,   *no stomach at all*
              And then its shanks,
They were as thin, as sharp an' sma',
              As cheeks o' branks.   *horse bridles*

'Guid-een' quo' I; 'Friend! Hae ye been   *Good evening*
 mawin,   *mowing*
'When ither folk are busy sawin?'   *sowing*
It seem'd to make a kind o' stan',
              But naething spak;   *said nothing*
At length, says I, 'Friend, whare ye gaun,
              'Will ye go back?'

It spak right howe – 'My name is *Death*,   *hollow*
'But be na' fley'd.' – Quoth I, 'Guid faith,   *afraid*
'Ye're maybe come to stap my breath;   *stop*
             'But tent me, billie;   *attend to, my man*
'I red ye weel, tak care o' skaith,   *advise, injury*
             'See, there's a gully!'   *large knife*

'Gudeman,' quo' he, 'put up your whittle,   *knife*
'I'm no design'd to try its mettle;
'But if I did, I wad be kittle   *would be likely*

95

'To be mislear'd,   misunderstood
'I wad na' mind it, no that spittle
        'Out-owre my beard.'

'Weel, weel!' says I, 'a bargain be't;
'Come, gies your hand, an' sae we're gree't;   give, so agreed
'We'll ease our shanks an' tak a seat,
        'Come, gies your news!
'This while ye hae been mony a gate,   have, many
        'At mony a house.'

'Ay, ay!' quo' he, an' shook his head,
'It's e'en a lang, lang time indeed
'Sin' I began to nick the thread,
        'An choke the breath:
'Folk maun do something for their bread,   must
        'An' sae maun *Death*.

'Sax thousand years are near hand fled   six
'Sin' I was to the butching bred,
'And mony a scheme in vain's been laid,
        'To stap or scar me;
'Till ane Hornbook's tae'n up the trade,
        'And faith, he'll waur me.   worst

'Ye ken John *Hornbook* i' the Clachan,   village
'Deil mak his king's-hood in a spleuchan!   entrails, tobacco
                                                            pouch
'He's grown sae weel acquaint wi' *Buchan*,   medical book
        'And ither chaps   other
'The weans haud out their fingers laughin,   children hold
        'And pouk my hips.   pluck

96

'See, here's a scythe, and there's a dart,
'They hae pierc'd mony a gallant heart;
'But Doctor *Hornbook*, wi' his art
                'And cursed skill,
'Has made them baith no worth a f–t,
                'D—n'd hae't they'll kill!

''Twas but yestreen, nae farther gaen,   last night
'I threw a noble throw at ane;
'Wi' less, I'm sure, I've hundreds slain;
                'But deil-ma-care!   devil
'It just play'd dirl on the bane,   knock, bone
                'But did nae mair.

'*Hornbook* was by, wi' ready art,
'And had sae fortify'd the part,
'That when I looked to my dart,
                'It was sae blunt,
'Fient haet o't wad hae pierc'd the heart   not a bit of it
                                        would
                'Of a kail runt.   cabbage stem

'I drew my scythe in sic a fury,   such
'I nearhand cowpit wi' my hurry,   tumbled
'But yet the bauld *Apothecary*   bold
                'Withstood the shock;
'I might as weel hae try'd a quarry
                'O' hard whin-rock.   hard

'E'en them he canna get attended,
'Altho' their face he ne'er had kend it,
'Just sh – in a kail-blade and send it,   cabbage leaf
                'As soon's he smells 't.
'Baith their disease, and what will mend it,
                'At once he tells 't.

97

'And then a' doctor's saws and whittles,
'Of a' dimensions, shapes, an' mettles,
'A' kinds o' boxes, mugs, an' bottles,
                'He's sure to hae;
'Their Latin names as fast he rattles
                'As A B C.

'Calces o' fossils, earths, and trees;   powders
'True Sal-marinum o' the seas;   sea salt
'The Farina of beans and pease,   vegetable meal
                'He has 't in plenty;
'Aqua-fontis, what you please,   fresh water
                'He can content ye.

'Forbye some new, uncommon weapons,
'Urinus Spiritus of capons;   urine
'Or Mite-horn shavings, filings, scrapings,
                'Distill'd per se;
'Sal-alkali o' Midge-tail clippings,   salt
                'And mony mae.'   more

                                                         Alas! The grave
'Waes me for Johnny Ged's Hole now'   digger
Quoth I, 'if that thae news be true!
'His braw calf-ward whare gowans grew,   enclosure for
                'Sae white an' bonie,   calves, daisies
'Nae doubt they'll rive it wi' the plew;   dig up, plough
                'They'll ruin Johnie!'

The creature grain'd an eldritch laugh   groaned, weird
And says, 'Ye needna yoke the pleugh.   plough
'Kirk-yards will soon be till'd eneugh,   enough
                'Tak ye nae fear:
'They'll a' be trench'd wi' mony a sheugh,   ditch
                'In twa-three year.

98

'Whare I kill'd ane, a fair strae-death,   death in bed
'By loss o' blood, or want o' breath,
'This night I'm free to tak my aith,   oath
              'That Hornbook's skill
'Has clad a score i' their last claith,   cloth, shroud
              'By drap and pill.   drop

'An honest Wabster to his trade,   weaver
'Whase wife's twa nieves were scarce weel-   fists
  bred,
'Gat tippence-worth to mend her head,   twopence
              'When it was sair;
'The wife slade cannie to her bed,   slid, carefully
              'But ne'er spak mair.

'A countra Laird had ta'en the batts   colic
'Or some curmurring in his guts,   murmuring
'His only son for Hornbook sets,
              'And pays him well,
'The lad, for twa guid gimmer-pets,   good young pet
              'Was Laird himsel.   ewes

'A bonie lass, ye kend her name,
'Some ill-brewn drink had hov'd her wame,   swelled, belly
'She trusts hersel, to hide the shame,
              'In Hornbook's care;
'Hom sent her aff to her lang hame   off, death
              'To hide it there.

'That's just a swatch o' Hornbook's way,
'Thus goes he on from day to day,
'Thus does he poison, kill, an' slay,
              'An's weel pay'd for 't;   and is well paid

99

'Yet stops me o' my lawfu' prey
            'Wi' his d—mn'd dirt!

'But hark! I'll tell you of a plot,
'Tho' dinna ye be speakin o't;   don't
'I'll nail the self-conceited Sot,
            'As dead's a herrin: next, bet,
'Niest time we meet, I'll wad a groat,   threepence Scots
            'He gets his fairin!'   just reward

But just as he began to tell,
The auld kirk-hammer strak the bell   struck
Some wee short hour ayont the twal   beyond twelve
            Which rais'd us baith: made . . . get up
I took the way that pleas'd mysel,
            And sae did Death.

Address to the Unco Guid, or the Rigidly Righteous

I

O ye wha are sae guid yoursel,   *so, good*
    Sae pious and sae holy,
Ye've nought to do but mark and tell
    Your Neebour's fauts and folly!   *neighbour's faults*

Whase life is like a weel-gaun mill,   *whose, well-going*
    Supply wi' store o' water,   *well-filled*
The heapet happer's ebbing still,   *hopper's*
    And still the clap plays clatter.   *clapper of the mill*

II

Hear me, ye venerable Core,
    As counsel for poor mortals;
That frequent pass douce Wisdom's door   *prudent*
    For glaikit Folly's portals;   *foolish*
I, for their thoughtless, careless sakes,
    Would here propone defences,
Their donsie tricks, their black mistakes,   *hapless*
    Their failings and mischances.

III

Ye see your state wi' theirs compared,
    And shudder at the niffer,   *comparison*
But cast a moment's fair regard,
    What maks the mighty differ;
Discount what scant occasion gave,
    That purity ye pride in,

101

And (what's aft mair than a' the lave)   often more, all, rest
    Your better art o' hiding.

IV

Think, when your castigated pulse
    Gies now and then a wallop,
What ragings must his veins convulse,
    That still eternal gallop:
Wi' wind and tide fair i' your tail,
    Right on ye scud your sea-way:
But, in the teeth o' baith to sail,   both
    It makes an unco leeway.   odd

V

See Social Life and Glee sit down,
    All joyous and unthinking,
Till, quite transmugrify'd, they're grown   transformed
    Debauchery and Drinking:
O would they stay to calculate
    Th' eternal consequences:
Or your more dreaded h–ll to state,
    Damnation of expences!

VI

Ye high, exalted, virtuous Dames,
    Ty'd up in godly laces,
Before ye gie poor Frailty names,
    Suppose a change o' cases;
A dear-lov'd lad, convenience snug,
    A treacherous inclination –
But, let me whisper i' your lug,   ear
    Ye're aiblins nae temptation.   perhaps

102

VII

Then gently scan your brother Man   criticize
    Still gentler sister woman;
Tho' they may gang a-kennin wrang,   go a little wrong
    To step aside is human:
One point must still be greatly dark,
    The moving *Why* they do it;
And just as lamely can ye mark,
    How far perhaps they rue it.

VIII

Who made the heart, 'tis *He* alone
    Decidedly can try us,
He knows each chord its various tone,
    Each spring its various bias:
Then at the balance let's be mute,
    We never can adjust it;
What's *done* we partly may compute,
    But know not what's *resisted*.

Chronology of Burns's Life

Year	Life
1759	Born at Alloway, near Ayr, 25 January, first child of Agnes and William Burns, tenant farmer
1765	Taught, with his brother Gilbert, by John Murdoch, hired as their instructor
1766	Father begins to farm Mount Oliphant, a 70-acre farm near Alloway
1768	Father continues his sons' education himself when Murdoch leaves. Agnes Burns shares with Robert many songs and stories
1772	Robert and Gilbert go to school in Dalrymple, four miles from Ayr
1773	Murdoch returns to teach English in Ayr. Burns studies French, English Grammar, Latin
1774	Writes his first song to impress a girl called Nelly
1777	Family move to Lochlie, a 130-acre farm near the village of Tarbolton, where Burns attends a dancing class
1780	With six friends forms The Tarbolton Bachelors' Club, a debating society
1781	Goes to Irvine to learn flax-making. He is inducted as a mason
1782	Returns to Lochlie when the flax shop is burned to the ground

Chronology of his Times

Year	Artistic Context	Historical Events
1759	Voltaire, *Candide* Haydn, First Symphony Johnson, 'Rasselas'	British Museum opens
1760	Macpherson, *Fragments of Ancient Poetry, Collected in The Highlands of Scotland*	Death of George II; succeeded by George III, his grandson
1764	Walpole, *The Castle of Otranto*	
1765	Percy, *Reliques of Ancient English Poetry*	
1766	Goldsmith, *The Vicar of Wakefield*	
1769		Birth of Napoleon Bonaparte
1769–70		James Cook's first voyage round the world
1770	Goldsmith, 'The Deserted Village'	First public restaurant opens in Paris
1773		Boston Tea Party: American protest against tea duty
1774	Goethe, *Sorrows of Werther*	First Congress of the 13 Colonies, except Georgia, meets at Philadelphia
1776	Smith, *Inquiry Into the Nature and Causes of the Wealth of Nations*	American Declaration of Independence
1778	Sheridan, *The School for Scandal*	
1781	Rousseau, *Confessions* Kant, *Critique of Pure Reason*	

Year	Life
1783	Begins his first Commonplace Book. He and Gilbert secretly arrange to lease Mossgiel, a farm near the village of Mauchline, to help the family's economic circumstances and their dying father
1784	Death of William Burns in February. The next month the family move into Mossgiel
1785	Meets Jean Armour at a Mauchline dance. He writes much poetry. 22 May, birth of Elizabeth, his daughter by Elizabeth Paton
1786	Relationships under much stress. April, proposals for *Poems, Chiefly In The Scottish Dialect* published; book itself is published at Kilmarnock on 31 July in an edition of 600 copies
1787	April, first Edinburgh edition of *Poems*. Makes a number of tours. Begins to contribute songs to James Johnson's *Scots Musical Museum* (1787–1803). Meets Mrs Agnes McLehose ('Clarinda'). 20 October, first London edition of *Poems*
1787–8	Much of this winter spent in Edinburgh
1788	Accepts Jean Armour as his wife, leases the farm of Ellisland, near Dumfries, and is commissioned as an Exciseman. From now on, writes more songs than poems
1789	Begins work in the Excise at a salary of £50 per annum
1790	Writes 'Tam o' Shanter'
1791	Gives up Ellisland in favour of full-time Excise work and moves to Dumfries
1792	Asked to contribute songs to George Thomson's *A Select Collection of Scottish Airs* (1793–1818)
1793	Second Edinburgh edition of *Poems* and first set of Thomson's *Select Collection*
1794	Appointed Acting Supervisor of Excise
1795	Joins in organizing Dumfries Volunteers. Severely ill with rheumatic fever
1796	21 July, dies at Dumfries

Year	Artistic Context	Historical Events
1783		England recognizes USA; first aerial voyages by hot-air and hydrogen balloons
1784		Vincent Lunardi, first balloon flight over England
1787	Mozart, Don Giovanni	
1788		Death of Charles Edward Stuart ('Bonnie Prince Charlie')
1789	Blake, Songs of Innocence	Fall of the Bastille: French Revolution; George Washington becomes President of USA
1790	Paine, The Rights of Man Burke, Reflections on the French Revolution	
1791	Boswell, The Life of Samuel Johnson, LL.D.	First ten amendments to USA Constitution
1792		French Republic established
1793		First Coalition against France; France declares war on Britain
1794	Blake, Songs of Experience	Beginning of friendship between Goethe and Schiller
1795		Speenhamland Act (Poor Law) wages supplemented by doles
1798	Wordsworth and Coleridge, Lyrical Ballads	